No Pain, No Gain
The Kevin Ward Story

No Pain, No Gain
The Kevin Ward Story

Dave Sampson and Kevin Ward

Vertical Editions

Copyright © Dave Sampson and Kevin Ward 2003

The right of Dave Sampson and Kevin Ward to be identified as the authors of this work has been asserted in accordance with the Copyright, Designs and Patents Act, 1988

All rights reserved. The reproduction and utilisation of this book in any form or by any electrical, mechanical or other means, now known or hereafter invented, including xerography, photocopying and recording, and in any information storage and retrieval system, is forbidden without the written permission of the publisher

First published in the United Kingdom in 2003 by Vertical Editions, Unit 4a, Snaygill Industrial Estate, Skipton, North Yorkshire BD23 2QR

ISBN 1-904091-05-9

www.verticaleditions.com

Cover design and typeset by HBA, York

Printed and bound by Cromwell Press Group, Trowbridge

Contents

Foreword - Great Britain
Foreword - Australia
Introduction

1.	The Young Pretender	14
2.	The Rebellious Years	26
3.	Wagon and Horses	31
4.	Super League - If Only…	41
5.	Dream Team	43
6.	A Worthwhile Adventure	48
7.	Big Mack	62
8.	Reflections	67
9.	Testing the Water	71
10.	Learning How to Win	81
11.	Laying the Ghost to Rest	93
12.	The Battle of Belle Vue	99
13.	Johnny Got It Wrong	104
14.	Unfair Tribunal	110
15.	A Cool Lager, a Final Lost	114
16.	Good Friday, Bad Friday	118
17.	Two Paths, Choosing the Right One	129
18.	A Night of Praise	134
19.	A Night of Nostalgia	138

Postscript 149
Appendix 152

Acknowledgements

Dave Sampson and Kevin Ward would like to thank all those who helped in the compilation of this book, notably Frank Poskitt for the information he has allowed us to use from his excellent publications, *A Little Bit about Stanley in Bygone Days* and *Mining and Pit Disasters*. To Len Garbutt the time honoured Castleford rugby historian whose detailed records were invaluable to this book. To Sig Kasatkin for his superb photographs. To the charismatic Ray French for his kind comments. To Sean Fagan for his help in Australia and the inspirational rugby league website he runs at: www.RL1908.com To Bill Bates who came to the rescue when we began to block. To our wives, Mavis and Margaret, for their loyal support. To our families for the encouragement they gave us. And especially to Rebecca Sampson for painstakingly deciphering the longhand story and typing it into a presentable manuscript.

Foreword
Great Britain

The best of British boxers invariably have to display their craft in America before they are acknowledged as truly great fighters. Leading footballers in England are forced to travel to Italy or Spain to achieve their ambitions and earn the right to be accorded the adulation they deserve. It is so with rugby league players who are only ranked above and beyond their fellow countrymen when they have toughed it out in the hardest 13 a side arena in the world, Australia.

Kevin Ward did just that as a guest player for the Manly Sea Eagles in 1987, helped them to a Grand Final success over the Canberra Raiders, and returned to take his rightful place among the hierarchy of props in world rugby. Like David Bolton, Cliff Watson, Tommy Bishop and Mal Reilly before him and, today, like Adrian Morley, his reputation is secure in both hemispheres. And rightly so!

An outstanding career with both St Helens and Castleford and a collection of seventeen Test caps, nine of which were gained following rough, tough physical clashes with the Australians, are testimony to Kevin's playing ability. But, as with most props, their size and aggression on the pitch often hides a more thoughtful and intelligent approach off it.

The title, *No Pain, No Gain* perfectly sums up Kevin's approach to eighty minutes of rugby league, whether it be in a Sea Eagles', a Tigers', or a Saints' jersey. However, throughout the pages of this biography the reader will note the serious, caring approach with which he tackles some of the issues of his era and of today.

A quiet, modest, and unassuming man off the field, Kevin was never afraid to stand up and be counted when the action in the middle became a little overheated. Neither is he afraid to say exactly what he thinks on the action that occurred off the field. *No Pain, No Gain* mirrors the big man himself – read it, and you will see just what it takes to become a hero in two hemispheres.

Ray French
League Weekly and BBC Sport

Foreword
Australia

Before his first match on a bright sunny May afternoon, perfect for rugby league at Brookvale Oval, Kevin was interviewed for the TV coverage. Squinting badly as he tried to shield the sun's glare, when he spoke I couldn't understand a word of it. Ward looked as unlikely a starter in Sydney rugby as ever seen.

Eighty minutes of rugby league later, I stood and applauded along with the rest of the Brookie Hill, we had a new hero. Coach Fulton had put Ward straight into first grade for a top-of-the-table showdown with Balmain. The Sea Eagles went into overdrive, winning 48-14. Ward's powerful runs up front gave the flashy Manly backs the space and time they needed. All of a sudden, 'Napper' Lyons was a masterful playmaker, 'Snoz' O'Connor was making breaks at will, 'Tinker' Williams was an accomplished finisher and 'Rambo' Ronnie Gibbs was running amok in the midfield.

Ward was interviewed after the 1987 Grand Final win. I still couldn't work out much of what he was saying. But by then it didn't matter, anything I needed to know about Kevin Ward was there on the football field to see, and it was all strength, commitment and unrelenting power. Those of us who sat on the SCG hill in the 37°C hot sun that day will attest to that.

It's a measure of the man's status in Australia that without exception, whenever anyone speaks of that last SCG Grand Final, they always mention, 'That pommy Kevin Ward, he was unbelievable!'

Sean Fagan
www.RL1908.com

Introduction

When my publisher, Karl Waddicor of Vertical Editions first approached me about writing Kevin Ward's biography, I hesitated, I thought: not another collier's son makes good story.

'It's been done before, it's played out.' I argued. This led to a lively debate.

'Dave you're backing away from the traditions that you champion.'

'I suppose Karl; this comes from an in built inferiority complex of being the son of a collier, a long line of them.'

'Yes but you advocate walk tall, be proud of your heritage.'

'Sure I do, but there are an awful lot of colliers, or sons or daughters of colliers who have made good in sport.'

'I agree Dave but Kevin has a place in history, he's one of the modern day elite band of rugby league players to emerge from the traditional coalfield heartlands of the sport, that should be justification enough.'

'I'm not arguing on the subject matter, I suppose I'm a little afraid of becoming repetitive.'

'Well, I think you need to look at the facts. First, you are lucky to come from a mining village that has produced thousands of tons of coal over many years, in fact long before the industrial revolution and so steeped in traditional values. And second, you are equally lucky that this very same village has produced many internationally renowned athletes over the last 100 years.'

'Well you may be right. I'll think about it.'

'I know I'm right, It's also a bonus that you have known him most of his life. I tell you Dave there are many people out there who would like to read about Kevin Ward, about Stanley village and the integral small Bottomboat community within its boundaries. How he grew in stature and standing within this parochial environment and then reached the highest pinnacles of rugby league. There will be a lot of people who gain enjoyment from his story having watched him in his prime and younger readers who will be inspired by his efforts and achievements. And you know the story probably better than anyone else of a man who deserves his place in the annals of sporting history.'

'Hmm, so if I wrote this book, what would the title be?'

'How about *No Pain, No Gain*? That would sum up Kevin's achievements.'

Kevin Ward made his debut on a Wednesday evening. The date: March 14th 1979. The match: Salford. The Red Devils at the Willows. This was to be the first of 316 appearances for Castleford his last match being April 22nd 1990 at Headingley on a cool bright Sunday afternoon. The result at Salford a 16 points to 5 defeat. Kevin was introduced from the subs bench to tread nervously onto a playing surface that had been graced by many immortalised legends of the past. But since the Willows was first opened on the 21st of December 1901 very few forwards were to, or had achieved more in performance or esteem from his peers than the consummately shy, angular, raw-boned Stanley lad. Certainly, his ignominious departure from Castleford was scant reward for his loyal service.

Once again as a sub, he graced Headingley for the last

time in his beloved Castleford colours and once again, Cas were on the losing end of an 18-24 score line. This however was not to be Kevin's swan song, the illustrious mighty St Helens saw in him a platform, from which they could launch a bid to wrest the dominance of Wigan and thus ended their search to replace Andy Platt, a £145,000 sale to Wigan some eighteen months earlier. Kevin had fourteen international appearances to his credit, though many pundits thought it should have been more. He also had two stints with Manly in his record, where, such was his prowess, he endeared himself to the Aussie public. And later at St Helens he was revered by the fans, which aptly reflected the impact he made when and wherever he played. He went on to play a further eighty-eight times for Saints and he gained further representative honours. When forced to retire due to a horrific leg fracture, Kevin had amassed a career total of 451 games.

This is his story.

1

The Young Pretender

The adage No Pain, No Gain, might seem a simplistic way of entitling this book but the truth is the words cover a multitude of aspects in a sportsperson's life. It is possibly modern terminology, but the concept has been with the human race for thousands of years. Take, for example, the soldiers of the Roman Empire. Yes, they were highly skilled, well-trained individuals, who were organised and stuck to a game plan but a large part of their success was due to their disciplined hard-working efforts to achieve a chosen objective. And in modern day sport the same concept holds true. Just look at what Wigan achieved in the 80s and 90s, no wonder at the advent of Super League they chose the name Warriors! Although to really put things in perspective, rugby players the world over should be deemed warriors. Indeed hard work coupled with part-time training honed the early rugby league player into a physical machine. However it was modern technological advances that gave us the Ellery Hanleys of this world, once described by a prominent British sports scientist as 'the epitome of perfection of an all round athlete in what is indisputably the most demanding team game in the world'. This wise respected professor went on to say, 'the demands on his body to peak so many times in one arduous year and yet maintain a weekly high standard also bordered on freakish'. The same professor had tested icons from all sports and completely independent of bias, he extolled the praises for Ellery. I recall informing the same man that I acknowledged his assessment of Ellery and agreed, he truly had become the ambassador of rugby, and a yardstick for budding athletes to emulate. But I told him Ellery is not alone, there are many more within our game who are equally deserving of respect. And while we as a nation simply have not for many years been able to produce enough of these heroes to enable us to consistently compete with Australia, we have nonetheless produced a notable few elite 'Super Warriors' of which Kevin Ward is undoubtedly one.

Kevin peaked at Castleford under the astute tutelage of Mal Reilly and his coaching regime, but what we really needed at that time were three more of his like. The Aussies were taking us on with four the stature of Kevin in the front row and a replacement bench with the likes of Tunks, Backo, Bella, Roach and Dunn. Now I do not want to appear unkind to Kevin's contemporaries, many of whom were accomplished and fearless competitors in their own right, yet in each case, apart from Waddell, Crooks and Skerrett, all were small in stature compared with their counterparts from down-under. The records show that Kevin and Lee Crooks performed well together in their international appearances, it's just a pity that they were split before they could have performed together for Cas. The split of these two international Trojans however benefited rugby league, with both making massive contributions to their respective teams. And if Lee was a little envious of Kevin's Wembley soiree against Wigan so soon after parting, he was able to balance the scales a year later when Cas also made an unsuccessful attempt to break the stranglehold of the Lancashire juggernauts in their fifth consecutive victory.

No Pain, No Gain, epitomises Kevin's dogmatic determination to reach the top. As a part-time pro, he toiled firstly in the mines then on the building sites and after these gruelling shifts he punished himself relentlessly. He regularly sweated buckets enduring the repetitive arduous weights programmes, the five-mile runs against the clock, the interval runs and a sprint programme worthy of an Olympic runner. But as the start of each season approached, all these painstaking aspects of the creation of the modern player were gelled. Skill drills, polishing ball control aligned with speed, strength and agility and finally topped off with motivational coaching to produce an awesome player ready to compete at the highest level. Kevin made these painful physical demands on himself year in year out. He played in 451 games and excelled at the highest level with Castleford, Manly, St Helens and Great Britain and no one is more entitled to call his story *No Pain, No Gain*.

Throughout the well documented history of the greatest game on earth, rarely has the word colossus been used to describe a sporting hero, however in the case of Kevin Ward, many opponents and respected scribes in both hemispheres would, did, and still do ascribe such a word befitting to Wardy, or 'the beast' to a chosen few. Now Kevin is a shy, unassuming giant of a man in equal measures of stature and persona, had he graced the high profile Super League era his fame would have known no boundaries. Unfortunately, for Kevin it can be said he was born too soon, he does however belong in that exclusive club of rugby icons pre-Super League, who had the attributes to be champions whatever the era.

I deem myself very privileged indeed to have known him

from an early age. I first noticed him as a twelve year old playing full back for his school team, a heavy boned but lithe boy with obvious talent. Several other boys of equal promise played alongside Kevin that day; Steve 'Blegsy' Hunter, who later in life signed for Bramley, Howard 'Bud' Budby who signed for Leeds and later Wakefield and Peter Harrison, son of former Wakefield and Batley prop Derek, who also joined Leeds. These four prodigies were friends on and off the pitch and what the Bowery Boys were to the slums of New York, these four were ringleaders of Stanley's equivalent.

Kevin's grandfather, Richard Westwood Ward, known locally as Dick, was also a professional rugby league player and thereby established a trait, which his grandson would follow. Born in Bottomboat, a small hamlet within the village of Stanley, it has been known since the early 18th century as the place where the ferryboat crossed the river Calder, linking Stanley with the village of Altofts. It appears in records as early as 1202 as Stanlie Bothum, and it is probable Richard Le Bothum took his title from the area inspiring Bothumboat, a derivative of Bottomboat as it stands today. The river Calder wends its way through the valley to the North Sea and running parallel along the valley is the A629, the old York to Wakefield highway known as the Aberford Road. Approximately one mile from junction 30 of the M62 and three miles before Wakefield is the turn off signposted Bottomboat, I should add the only turn off, as it is one way in and the same way out. Long gone are the ferry, the school, the working men's club, all but one pub and quite recently the chapel, having sadly closed its doors for the last time. I can recall an old village character from my youth, Harry Field, a hard, tough yet respected man and sire to an international boxer, Ernie Field who turned pro and fought for the British title. 'David,' he said, 'do you know why Bottomboat has always maintained a population of 200 inhabitants?'

'I haven't a clue Harry.'

'Because every time a new babe was born, someone had to leave.'

Harry was tough as an old boot but with a warm endearing sense of humour and like many Bottomboaters, not a man to cross.

When I questioned Kevin about his grandfather, Kevin refers me to his own father Alan. 'You'll have to ask me dad,' he says. Alan is instantly responsive to my question. 'Well David his rugby career was ending when I was born in 1930 so by the time I was of any age to really know him, his playing days were long gone and he rarely spoke of em. Mostly I recall he was a full back and understudy so to speak of the great Charlie Pollard, a two time tourist of the twenties era. Dad signed on for Wakefield Trinity in 1925 as a nineteen year old from Stanley Nibs as they were known then, he went on to make 85 first team appearances, kicking two goals and scoring six tries, his final season being 1930-31, the year I was born. Who knows, maybe that's why he retired. I can recall him telling me that he was paid thirty bob and a pound of tripe for winning cos it seems a director at that time had a butchers shop.'

Alan, like his father and his grandfather was raised in Bottomboat but he knew little of rugby league. In the year that he was born, Bottomboat placed themselves firmly on the football map winning the Leeds League Cup, the Leeds Hospitals Cup and the Wakefield Challenge Cup. Dick involved himself with the many talented soccer players of this tiny hamlet, so it is little wonder that Alan was groomed into the world of the round ball. Alan showed enough skill and promise to be picked up by Methley who competed in a higher league, and for a teenager working in a clog factory; drawing an additional fifteen shillings a week must have made life a little easier.

When Alan reached eighteen, he left the clog factory and went to till the rich fertile soil beside the banks of the Calder for a local market gardener. Alan fondly remembers these times and graphically recalls the winters when the frosts came and froze the bottom land, permanently flooded by about two inches of water. This expanse became a Mecca for visitors to enjoy the safe spacious acres of ice-skating, mostly locals in clogs, but many from surrounding villages. During this era following the Second World War, communities became more adventurous, less parochial. But in contrast it was often claimed that many people were born in Bottomboat and the first time they ventured out was in a pine box up to Stanley cemetery. Alan was one of those who ventured out and it was inevitable that on the many Saturday night sojourns he would meet a girl and fall in love. He met and courted Normanton born Doreen and they soon married in 1956 at Wakefield registry office and then returned to Stanley British Legion Club for the reception. At the time, it may have all seemed a whirlwind to some, but it proved not a moment too soon as the British Legion Club blew down in a storm a few days on.

Alan and Doreen settled into a new prefab on Ferry Lane, Alan had ceased tilling the riverside soil, he followed the trend and went down the pit. Then on August 15th 1956, Doreen presented Alan with their first son, Steven, born in the grandeur of Walton Hall Hospital, a former stately home, then less than twelve months later on the 5th of August 1957, Kevin arrived, ten and a half pounds at birth, a sure indication of the size he was later to attain. He was born in their cosy little prefab after which the local GP, Doctor Merrick, paid a visit - as Alan and Doreen tell it - to answer a few pertinent questions on family planning. Doctor Merrick answered in his usual forthright manner, 'Keep going while the fires are still hot.' Alan and Doreen took his advice and in November 1958 Janice was born followed by Andrea in January 1961, David in January 1963 and finally Neil in September 1965. Not surprisingly, the prefab soon proved too small, so when the opportunity came, Alan and Doreen moved their family to a new council house on nearby St Peters Crescent. From these humble beginnings, Alan and Doreen were able to provide a stable environment.

The wages on the land could never have sustained such a family, but moving from the fresh air environment of farming into the dusty choking depths of a coal mine was a culture shock to Alan but it was a case of needs must. His forbears had mined the rich Silkstone seam in the old inhospitable ancient workings of two now closed and capped Bottomboat and Parsons shafts. The Newmarket Silkstone had replaced these decrepit relics where many, young and old alike, had lost their lives, all attributed to the work of God or in his name. The Newmarket Silkstone was much safer and more modern; however, it was a tough start to 1955. It was during his early mining days that Alan was subjected to mithering from his fellow work mates to try his hand at rugby league so Alan switched from soccer to rugby, turning out at stand off half for two seasons with Stanley Rangers where history reports his talent was exceptional.

Alan enjoyed his rugby and reminisces warmly of such times however his first love beckoned him and he played out the latter days of his sporting career with the local Victoria football side. At this time, Steven and Kevin were fast growing youths and although brothers, they were like chalk and cheese - both creative natured but in vastly differing ways. Steven had artistic talent and loved to work a pencil or brush, whereas Kevin's affinity was for a soccer ball, hour after hour, day after day he would spend his spare time dribbling and perfecting ball skills. He rarely considered rugby in those days apart from the odd compulsory school match, but his ability did not go unnoticed, it was simply that his all-consuming love was with soccer. The many hours Kevin spent perfecting the art of controlling the ball with his head and feet benefited him to such an extent that he starred with his school team throughout all the age groups and then he achieved representative honours with his district team. At Stanley Secondary School at this time, there was an abundance of gifted boys at both soccer and rugby, Kevin excelled at both playing full back and stand off at rugby and as centre forward at soccer. He also excelled at cricket as an all rounder with the rare distinction of being opening bat and opening left arm fast bowler. In fact, such were the capabilities of Kevin and his young school chums on the cricket pitch that in the summer of 1971 they won the coveted Robinsons League Champions Shield. The team included good pal Pete Harrison, who later signed for Leeds RLFC and Gerald 'Jez' King who, after showing great promise at soccer as a teenager, like Kevin, changed codes and signed for Dewsbury RL. Also present was Chuckie Myton who played for many seasons with Stanley Rangers and now sits on the coaching staff. Indeed these boys were indicative of the amount of sporting talent to emerge from the Stanley area. Other notable athletes include Barry Hoban who achieved Olympic status in 1960 in Rome. Such was his prowess in the world of cycling he amassed eight Tour De France stage wins, a present day British record. Barry, the son of a miner, now enjoys a comfortable lifestyle in Belgium a far cry from the Lime Pit Lane council house of his youth. Top jockey George Duffield MBE achieved fame in the sport of kings. Having grown up in Stanley, he has ridden to victory in over two thousand races and currently stands at tenth in the All-Time British Winners list. My own niece, Denise Ramsden achieved fame as a sprinter, representing Britain at the 1976 Montreal Olympics. She was born and lived all her life in the Stanley area until her recent untimely death. And there are many others too including soccer players Don and George Howe, boxer Ernie Fields and my own son Dean Sampson. All emerged from the same coalfield environment, all showed promise at an early age, all possessed inherent talent and Kevin was no exception.

Kevin was approached by Sheffield Wednesday, at that time a giant of a club and trials were arranged. Alan was a very proud man at this time, his mum too but the unpredictable side of Kevin was beginning to emerge. He was physically very mature but in reality was still a kid, and the lure of the good life after a hard day's work in the pit were unwelcome distractions to all who knew him - except to Kevin himself. Kevin had completed his education at the age of fifteen, yet although his sporting prowess gained him high regard with teachers and fellow pupils, his lack of interest in academic achievement coupled with classroom antics brought him under much scrutiny. On one occasion in the woodwork classroom, a cork sandpaper block whizzed across the room towards the doorway. Its intended recipient ducked just in time, the missile continued on its path toward a now open door, the midday sun obstructed by the stocky powerful figure of the notorious Mr Alan Parker who was struck in the chest. 'Ward,' he bellowed, 'into the stock room NOW!' A cocky Kevin strode across the now silent room where he took his first trip into the pain den, a few minutes later a more humble Kevin emerged and gingerly made his way back to his workbench. A size 11 white plimsoll had stood the test of time, a few swinging whacks from this intimidating weapon would humble as many youngsters in the ensuing years as it had in the past - well at least up to the banning of corporal punishment in schools. But Kevin was long gone by then, although not before falling foul of Alan Parker and his colleague, Tony Proffit, on many more occasions. One such time was when these two gentlemen made a lunch time midweek visit to the Ship Inn whose licensee happened to be none other than myself. Pleasantries were exchanged before the question was put to me, 'Have you been getting any visits from our boys David?'

'If they so much as step over my threshold I'll send them packing, I'll not serve kids in here,' I replied,

'Well David, they're getting ale somewhere up here in Lee Moor and there are only two pubs so we'll not trouble you again.'

A few minutes later four youths, unknown to me at that time, came scampering out of the Miners Arms opposite with Alan and Tony in hot pursuit. I recall thinking to myself those lads were in for some pain. Eventually, as in any community, the names of the culprits filtered back into my pub - Ward, Budby, Hunter, Harrison - it's ironic I suppose that they all played professional rugby a few years on and it's probably from beginnings such as this that all have turned out to be characters in their own right. But how Kevin's parents coped feeding, clothing and raising such a family is testimony to their commitment. Doreen ensured that all would each in turn, in their own way, make her and Alan proud and she freely admits to this day that feeding her family kept her busy with cooking and baking. The pleasure derived watching them consume such lovingly prepared homemade dishes was ample reward enough, nor was she adverse to Kevin's friends sharing. And she can still shed a tear of laughter at the blackberry and apple pie Kevin, Johnny Milner and Pete Harrision fettled in one sitting. 'They blooming well cleaned the pattern off the plate - a full pie, a third each.'

One thing Kevin learned at an early age was that taking knocks both physically and mentally hurt but he was always positive coming off the back of such events, even if the disappointment was of his own making. Kevin at eighteen years old was a proverbial local soccer star turning out both Saturday afternoon and again Sunday mornings. He played in a very successful Travellers team in the Tetley Sunday League and as this particular season was drawing to a close, the team had reached four cup finals and all were to be played within a period of fourteen days. Kevin had starred all season banging home goal after goal with monotonous regularity - he was to Stanley what John Charles had been to Leeds United. Now the coach of this Sunday side was none other than my brother Malcolm, who after finishing his own rugby league career, took up the reigns of coaching and training young enthusiastic village lads in the opposite code. Malcolm had played soccer during his school days and still held an affinity to the round ball game. He proclaimed that because there were four finals to play, out of fairness he would make sure that even the reserves got to start at least one final; I guess rotation is the modern equivalent. Kevin was earwigging on this conversation between Malc and his assistant Melvyn

Castle and on hearing this turned to his fellow players and he in turn was overheard to utter, 'Well he can't drop me.' Silly lad, Malcolm had taken it on board and kept it to himself, then on the Sunday morning, calm as you please, announced Derek Halmshaw was starting and Kevin would be sub. That was an early shock to Kevin but something our Malc argued would stand him in good stead for the future. Derek went on in Kevin's position and within five minutes, he scored the opening goal. At this point Kevin was prowling and growling up and down the touchline, mumbling and pleading for a run on but Malc made him sweat. Then with the game finely poised, he gave him the nod, Kevin duly obliged heading home the winner, back in his role as king of the castle but he later confided it was a lesson learned.

The team lost only one of the four finals that year and only by the odd goal, a record that stood for twenty-five years.

2

The Rebellious Years

On leaving school, Kevin embarked on a new major chapter in his life. It was natural that he followed his dad Alan into the mine, so at the age of fifteen he went down the pit. Kevin, however, was never too enamoured to a working life on the coalface, he thought of it as just a way to earn money. Oh he could cope with the hard graft and drudgery of the day after day banal lifestyle, 'Simply because it was a means to an end.' But like many others, he was drawn into a culture that had been in existence for generations, when come Friday, draw your wage, pay your board, then go to the pub. On Saturday a game of soccer, the high point of his week, followed by a more serious drinking session, usually culminating with all the gang heading for town and a late night drinking den. On occasions, a bit of a ruck with lads from other villages broke out, usually over an equally inebriated young girl. Fortunately it was rare that anyone was seriously hurt in those days, the drug fuelled culture and the violent crime related antics had not yet emerged. Kevin's physical stature, even at this tender age, his imposing stance and his renown on the soccer field from village to village, helped in keeping his nose clean. He was already attaining respect from his peers and as in most small close-knit communities, word travelled fast, 'Don't mess with Wardy'. The truth of it was Kevin wanted only to be left to his own devices. He was an affable lad from an affable family who had (and still does have) an easy-going approach to his life, however as with many a drink fuelled teenager, he didn't survive these halcyon years without the odd incident and the occasional brush with the law. Never violent but often funny, on one such late night event Kevin somehow found himself in the upper branches of a Wakefield town centre tree. A concerned inspector appeared and asked the proverbial, 'And what do you think you're doing?'

'I'm a fucking monkey, I'm just hanging around,' came the flippant reply.

'Well how on earth did you get up there?'

'I just swung.'

'Oh like a monkey I suppose.'

'Yes officer.'

'Well bloody well swing back down again, now!'

Kevin obliged and was escorted the whole five yards to Wood Street Police Station for what he insisted later was a cup of coffee and a warning to his future behaviour. The inspector told him, 'If you want to climb trees at two-thirty in the morning go into the park and not outside the police station front door.'

Peter Harrison, a pal throughout all those early years, recalled many great times they spent together, whether as part of a bigger group of mates or just the two of them. Later Peter was to meet Joy, Kevin married Margaret and as happens the two lads drifted apart. Ironic that both girls were teachers - a very unlikely combination, Peter readily agrees.

'You know Dave there were so many unprintable escapades, who would have believed how our lives have evolved and where we are now. Most incidents were mischievous, high-spirited things, we rarely got into any serious trouble, we were too good-natured and believe it or not, respectful of others. We had well balanced upbringings yet I do admit we lived day-today with little thought, if any, for the future. I recall during our last term at school, none of us were academic superstars so we decided to take the afternoon off. This particular morning, the careers officer had visited and our mate, Bleggsy, decided to ring Newmarket Colliery to enquire if they had any job application forms. "No but you can get them from Lofthouse," said the manager. So the three of us then knocked on the headmaster's door and sought permission to be excused lessons that afternoon in order to walk to Lofthouse Colliery and sign up. Of course, we had no intention of doing any such thing. However, the headmaster, Mr Wilson, was sharper than we gave him credit for, he immediately phoned the colliery manager and told him to expect us in an hour. We left his office blaming each other for coming up with such a hair-brained scheme. When we reached Lofthouse Colliery after a two-mile trek, the manager was waiting for us. "Fill these forms in lads. Harrison you can start at Lofthouse first Monday in August, Ward and Hunter you can start at Newmarket the same day. Welcome to the National Coal Board lads, oh and don't be late, 6 o'clock on the dot." Each of us were in shock, what we planned as a lazy afternoon, skiving off school, sunbathing on the banks of the Calder had gone horribly wrong.'

I know when Kevin thinks back to his time as a teenager he has happy memories of playing soccer on Saturday and Sunday afternoons, which I suppose is no surprise given the number of trophies he won with Stanley United. But my brother Malc and I felt he could perform even better at rugby league having watched him play the odd game. So we spoke with him suggesting he give it a try and Kevin readily agreed. He immediately proved a revelation with Stanley Rangers, an instant hit, he was a ball players dream as Barry Johnson at

Castleford was later to find out. But much of the credit is due to Malcolm as he knew that Kevin taking up the sport would be a big loss to his soccer side, yet he unselfishly reassured him to concentrate on rugby and give it his best shot. Needless to say it was not long before scouts were turning up on the touchline and Kevin followed his boyhood pals Peter Harrison and Howard Budby for trials with Leeds - much to my displeasure!

He was showing enough promise to sign immediately as a professional, yet in the trials he found himself being frozen out by more senior players. Malc and I watched him play against Wakefield Trinity at Belle Vue where Kevin received only two passes all game whilst standing wide out in the centre position.

'What the hell were you out wide all the game for?' I asked.

'Stan McHugh told me to stand there,' came the reply.

'You've been set up,' I said, 'forget the trials, come back to Stanley on Saturday next, I'll play with you and if you do the business I will see if I can get you signed somewhere.'

I mentioned Kevin up at my club, Bramley, and I rang Wakefield and Castleford, then Chuck Hardisty turned up from Cas and Kevin did the rest. He played to his potential and although still raw in the finer points of the game, he showed enough ability to get Chuck's attention. The following Tuesday night the Castleford board met and on the recommendation of Alan Hardisity, discussed signing Kevin who with myself was waiting in the bar under the stand. Mal Reilly approached me, he had obviously been briefed by Alan and I assured him that Kevin would make it. I proceeded to propose a contract for Kevin, Mal returned to the boardroom and re-emerged a few minutes later. 'David, how sure are you about this lad?'

I didn't hesitate, 'He can go right to the top, I'm sure, I'll stake my name on him.'

Mal returned to the boardroom and a few minutes later

came back out smiling. 'It's agreed,' he said.

'You won't regret it Mal.'

'I certainly hope not, it's a record signing on fee for a junior at Castleford.'

Kevin received his cheque for the princely sum of £1,000, a down payment on a £3,000 contract. He signed the necessary forms and we both went out for a celebratory tipple. Next morning I received a phone call from Kevin. 'I've lost the cheque,' he said. I can't repeat my words but I assured him I'd take care of it. I then rang the chairman, Phil Brunt and explained what had happened. 'Well David, the last man who lost his signing on cheque at this club was Keith Hepworth, so if that's an omen and he turns out half as good, it will do for me.' Phil in turn agreed to take care of it but later that day Kevin rang me and rather sheepishly admitted he had now found it.

'Where was it?' I asked.

'Under the corner of the carpet, my mother found it.'

'Well tear it up, there's another one coming in the post.' I also explained what the chairman had said about Keith Hepworth.

'Who is Keith Hepworth?' he asked (such had been Kevin's devotion to soccer, he'd never heard of Castleford's international scrum half).

'Heppy, Heppy.' I exclaimed.

'Who him that sings with the Kalahari Bushmen?'

'Forget it Kevin just enjoy your training and always go for gold. I'll see you later.'

'Okay,' he answered, 'oh and thanks.'

I've treasured those words ever since.

3

Wagon and Horses

During the many hours I've recently spent with Kevin gleaning information sufficient to enable me to write his story, I found the process much easier as we relaxed over a pint or two - and sometimes more. Now as a young man, Kevin had the ability to consume alcohol in large quantities without too dramatic a character change or damage to his physical make up. He simply relaxed very easily and quickly as a result of the introduction of amber nectar into his massive imposing frame. His already affable nature would become more transparent thus putting all he came into contact with at instant ease. And more recently, the same amber nectar also seemed to stimulate his memory cells with only the slightest hint or trigger word from myself. The recollections would then come flooding forth, each one triggering another until I had to cease proceedings for a brief respite, thus enabling me to update my notes. Now I know my publisher thinks I'm some kind of Luddite because I write all my notes and manuscripts in long hand, never using a keyboard, and although slow and laborious, it can have its advantages. For instance after a few pints, the many stories, yarns and facts that spill from Kevin with a machine gun-like rat-tat-tat, well the pen allows me to note down trigger words that will later allow me to tap into my memory bank and recall his comments almost word for word. Another writer, let's say a more proficient scribe, would probably use a laptop or tape recorder and I'm sure Kevin would find both intimidating as he's a shy sort and mistrustful of strangers. And besides which, after a few pints with Kevin, they would probably forget to turn the tape recorder on! But I have been close friends with Kevin since he first entered my pub back then, the Ship Inn. At that time, he was a tall angular raw-boned seventeen year old who blushed with embarrassment and fired an aggressive retort of 'coarse I am' in reply to my question of was he old enough to be in the pub. That was thirty years ago when neither he nor I could have ever foreseen his glittering career then ahead of him. Or the fact as I now open the door to the Wagon and Horses on Lake Lock Road, Stanley, that I was about to embark on the adventure of retelling his life story. A fitting tribute to him and an honour for me.

Armed with a 240 page writing pad and two pens we stepped forward towards the bar and although I deliberately try to avoid buying the first round, I find myself handing one of the three fivers I have in my pocket to a lovely young barmaid. The few coppers change I receive makes me realise that neither Kevin or myself will make much money from this exercise, but as with my own book *Fast Lane To Shangri-La* and my son Dean's *My Shangri-La*, the camaraderie, the fun reliving the events and the satisfaction that a publisher deems us worthy of investment, should and is taken into account. It can also be construed as another honour, a tribute to our once tiny village, for Stanley has turned out more than its share of talent deserving of such accolades. As Kevin and I sit in the corner, he pauses and heaves such a sigh. 'It is some years since I've been in here Sammy.' The mere fact that Kevin refers to me as Sammy indicates he is at ease; this is one of his early stomping grounds for the Wagon was, during Kevin's teens, the headquarters of Stanley United where he many times starred at centre forward. And despite distractions from the odd few customers, well wishers who hadn't seen Kevin for many a year, we start to make progress. Then one of the locals, Dave Alexander comes over, fresh pint in hand. 'Nah then Joey,' he says, greeting Kevin.

'Ey-up Dog.' Kevin replies. A few more pleasantries continue understood only by such as myself as a totally relaxed Kevin meets the dialogue head on. I realise it is two-thirty and time for the Leeds versus St Helens match, we move into the big room and I am surprised, as is Kevin, at the sparsity of the audience. Kevin spies a Leeds fan in his blue and gold replica shirt. 'Saints by twenty points,' he says utterly confident and giving an indication that he still carries a torch for the club he performed for eighty-nine times when many thought him well past his best.

It's often said that Castleford made a mistake in letting Kevin go, but at thirty-three years old the £70,000 on offer was understandably too good to refuse. Added to which, Kevin wasn't seeing eye to eye with Darryl Van de Velde, so it's not surprising they accepted the deal. But Castleford's loss was Saints' gain, although only just because it was almost Hull KR who were the recipient of Kevin's coveted signature. Kevin tells the story of how he nearly moved east before finally heading west.

'My wife Margaret dropped me off at a prearranged meeting point in Cottingham near Hull when suddenly a black Mercedes came tearing round the corner and screeched to a stop. The rear door flew open Mafia-style, and in the back is sat Len Casey. He shouts, "Get in Kevin," then the car speeds off, being driven by none other than Phil Lowe and I knew him well because he'd also played for Manly in Sydney. At this stage I was leaning towards Hull KR, the money was very tempting, and my father-in-law lived there, but I felt it was fair to still listen to St Helens before making a final decision. But when Saints invited me over, well, you couldn't fail to be impressed by the set up, even though the money on offer was less. Then I thought about the Saints team sheet and that finally swung it for me. I mean, you don't often get the chance to play in a team of that quality.'

It is indicative of Kevin's prowess that those names on the team sheet who he held in high regard were players, who in the not too distant future, would cheer in unison at the announcement that Kevin was joining their ranks. It lifted the dressing room gloom just before a big game. The big fella passed his fitness test and soon joined players of tremendous quality such as George Mann, Roy Haggerty, Bernard Dwyer and Shane Cooper. In turn they too were both elated and relieved, such was Kevin's presence needed at Knowsley Road.

So back to the pub. Kevin and I watched the Leeds V St Helens game and we both agreed it was as good as we had seen for a long time. Referee Russell Smith was on top form, all but eradicating any messing about at the tackle and play the ball and it certainly added to the spectacle. A few friends then joined us including two Stanley old faces, Griss Ansell and Rusty Gardner. Griss immediately claimed it was he who introduced Kevin to rugby league.

Kevin responded, 'I was sat playing dominoes with Bleggsy Hunter when somebody came in and said Stanley

Rangers were short. We had no soccer match, no money and we were bored so we said why not.'

'Yes but it was me who put you through the gaps when all the big professional clubs came to watch,' Griss said.

At this point Neil, another mate, chimed in. 'It were Dave who was playing on permit from Bramley who put Kevin through gaps.'

I halted proceedings, 'Alan Hardisty came to watch Kevin and recommended him to Cas because he confronted me after the game and that's the truth. As for who put him through all those gaps, well I think Griss should have that honour and I'll put it in the book for posterity's sake.'

'By hell you're a good un Sammy,' Griss said.

Kevin was now the centre of attention, word had spread that he was in the pub and many wanted to shake his hand. Former colliers shared memories, anecdotes, and tales of days long gone. Some brought a sigh of sadness others had us rolling with laughter. And although Kevin did not stay too long down the mine - a wise move I remind him - he is still fiercely loyal and comments that he misses some of his old mates.

My son Dean then joined the troop and the conversation moved onto coaching. 'There's too much inconsistency between the rule book and fact,' Kevin interjected, 'David Waite must go nuts every time he sees the blatant disregard of the rules at the scrums and play the ball.'

'I agree,' Dean replies, 'and with Sky analysing every aspect of the game frame by frame, it's time the powers that be clamped down because we'll never get near the Aussies if we don't clean our act up in the domestic game.'

Kevin and I then reminisce seeing an old video of a very famous but already bent Aussie referee penalising a young enthusiastic Malcolm Reilly for an incorrect play the ball, the ref ruling that Mal's body wasn't directly facing the opponents' goal line; it caused a furore in the British camp. It was, to say the least, the height of pedantry committed by a confirmed pedagogue. That was almost forty years ago so could we say they were a dying breed? Certainly not, in fact in years gone by such officials were a rarity. Sergeant Major Clay may have been controversial but never pedantic. Fred Lindop whose equally authoritarian approach was often mistaken for arrogance, when in truth, it was self-confidence. Was he pedantic? Never, although he was wrong occasionally. The truth of the matter is that apart from the biff and bash of the old game, the basics were applied in general, more correctly, all be it slightly slower. Players complied more with the basics and the practice of referees dominating and effecting the outcome of a game was much rarer. Kevin makes the point that Colin Morris, a perfectly good referee ended up being downgraded and pilloried for his honest, yet over zealous mannerisms. It was tough on Colin, he came to the fore when application to the basics was on the decline and cheating the rules was becoming acceptable. Eagle-eyed Colin is valiantly trying to make a comeback in the modern game but I bet he cringes at the many times he has to turn a blind eye for the wrong reasons.

If one takes a look at the rule book, the law on the play the ball states something to the effect of, 'On completing the process of tackling an opponent and his progress is deemed complete the tacklers must immediately roll away.' It doesn't say in rotation of numbers, i.e. one, two, three or four with the last tackler using the tackled players body to push himself up. It quite clearly states the tacklers must roll away or peel off or let go in unison and as quickly as possible. Now the average number of penalties for laying on in Super League is say four per team per game, and the average number of tackles made per team per game is say 150. Taking these facts into account, I'm certain there are coaches out there who instruct their players to play the percentages. No doubt they will have analysed the referee for each match and so the poor old part-time ref has no chance in the modern full-time game.

The next issue is the tackled player, he is coached to rise to his feet as quickly as possible, even to the point of appearing to have an epileptic fit or suffering from St Vitus's dance; he wants to milk a penalty. Then on rising he lunges forward off the mark throwing the ball through his legs simultaneously. In the book he is supposed to raise himself onto the flats of his feet, place the ball on the ground and play the ball with his foot in a rear direction. For the sake of expediency, all the basic simple procedure is thrown out of the window and the mishmash that results in the modern concept of continuity of play is a farce. I wholly sympathise with the referees; with so many penalties that could be awarded just appertaining to one facet of play, well potentially we would never get a match finished!

Then Kevin points out, 'We're letting the game get sloppy and the coaches relish stretching the rules at every opportunity. A simplistic approach has sufficed for over a century, I'm not advocating live in the past, but a knock on is a knock on, it's not complicated and doesn't need complicating. A bent scrum feed is accepted as the norm, also it saddens me that some of the basic disciplines have become so slack and yet they're now accepted as the norm by the new converts to our game. People who have been brought up in Super League stare if some old wag shouts, "He never played that", it's our own fault, we are pandering to new fans and players by sacrificing the old standards.'

Griss intervenes, 'Yes, we lost our pits and our colliers and now we are losing the game that we love. Oh and by-the-way it's your round Kevin.'

'You've got to be joking,' Kevin replies.

'Once a tight git, always a tight git,' Rusty comments.

The banter then continues with each member of the now well-inebriated group trying to outdo the other with long forgotten tales. Black Dog tells one. 'I remember going back down the pit one Monday morning - first cage down't shaft after the weekend and we all were suffering hangovers. As the cage plummeted downwards we were all silent then young Tommy yelled out to break the ice, "Oh roll on next Friday" then the deputy says to him, "Tommy you're wishing your life away lad," so Tommy replied, "Well in that case I wish it were last Friday."' This brings a round of raucous laughter and sadly an end to the afternoon. As I walk home, I estimate that I have gleaned enough for at least a couple of thousand words, then I quickly calculate if the book is say 70,000 words then that will mean I will need thirty-five sessions at eight pints a session and the sum total will be 280 pints at a cost of £560. But if every session is as enjoyable as today has been, I will deem it money well spent.

Kevin walks with me as far as our house, it is during this brief stroll I make one last attempt to glean a few more of his thoughts. 'Any other little anecdotes you can offer me Kevin?' I ask.

'Yes,' he asserts, a large smile breaking across his face, which indicates another humorous revelation. I am attentive, pen in hand, eager to transcribe another hilarious occurrence in his distinguished career. He continues, 'it was when you were coach Dave, it was St Helens at Knowsley Road in a league match, things were getting a bit hot, it was a close game.'

'Yes I remember Kevin, we lost 14-6.'

'Well you know how fiery Roy Haggarty could get.'

'Yes his face would turn crimson with a sudden rush of blood.'

'Well Roy and Johnny Fifita were having a right old ding-dong throughout, it was the middle of the second half, Roy had driven the ball up and Johnny made one of his Tongan kamikaze special hits as only he could. Fortunately for Roy he ducked just in time. Johnny sailed over the top and I took Roy low. When Roy raised himself to play the ball, he stared over my shoulder at Johnny and told him he was a lunatic. So I turned just in time to see an equally fired up Johnny Fifita indicate with his finger across his throat in a slashing motion and snarling, "Next time I cut off your fucking head." He looked really mad and his eyes were bulging from the sockets. Roy looked shocked, he turned to the home bench and half-heartedly pleaded, "I think he means it."'

I had to laugh at Kevin's recollection. I was there but I had forgotten the incident; it was close to the touchline directly between the two dugouts. One of the Barrow brothers on the Saints bench turned to me and said, 'Hey Sammy has he got a machete in his shorts?'

'No,' I answered, 'but if he hits Roy with what he does have in his shorts Roy's in serious trouble.'

Kevin and I had a good laugh recalling the event. Then I told him the story of when I once asked Johnny which of the South Pacific Islanders were the governors. Johnny paused for a moment, then he patriotically said, "When Tongan get

No Pain, No Gain

into lead canoe, everybody else fuck off." I suppose there was some bias in there somewhere, but who was I to argue. Kevin and I said our goodbyes and promised to meet again the following week.

4

Super League - If Only...

Super League was made for Kevin Ward, not my words but from the man himself: 'I always took pride in my fitness, I always did extra without being asked, and I don't mean to undermine present day players, but playing twenty minutes in each half, well I could have continued until I was forty years old. Added to which, when competitive scrums vanished, the energy saved could be directed into other parts of the game like taking the defensive line up quicker and fighting to play the ball earlier. And I don't want to sound boastful but with the extra benefit of full-time training, well me and many that I played alongside would have given any Super League team a run for their money.'

'Yes,' I replied, 'and it helps with the dietary advances they have now.'

'Oh well that's a contentious subject with me Dave.'

'Why?'

'Well for one thing, the no drink culture would do my head in and while it's a sensible approach for kids coming into the game, in my case a total ban on alcohol would have definitely proved counter productive. Back then I would see players the night before a big game sipping diluted orange with faces as long as a wet weekend, supposedly preparing for the match. Well in my opinion that's tripe; players should be allowed to enjoy themselves and if that means going for a pint or two then so be it, and that way they can relax and then be more committed when called on to knuckle down. I personally always had a few pints, it was my way, I slept like a log, but I'm not saying a player should go out and get pissed, I'm talking moderation so don't misquote me.' (When Kevin says don't misquote me he means it.)

He goes on, 'It was the Aussies who introduced the orange juice culture and I never took it on board - probably to their annoyance when I was over there but that didn't matter to me. I don't need someone from Sydney or Brisbane to tell me that on the morning of the game I have to stuff myself with great dollops of pasta when what I want is my traditional English breakfast and a pot of tea. If I didn't perform doing it my way then they might have cause to complain. But look at the facts, in eleven seasons with Castleford, I only subbed ten times and I don't feel I have to justify my career or attitude. I was always aware, at least when I reached my mid twenties and married, that my behaviour should be that of a professional, but if the other guy wanted to sip orange and guzzle pasta so be it. Anyway, kids coming into the game now are indoctrinated into behaviour and diets but if they believe it makes them better players than their predecessors, then that's sad.'

'Hmm, you might have a point there Kevin.'

5

Dream Team

Kevin and I spoke at length about including a dream team in this book and although I had included my team of stars in my autobiography a couple of years ago, I must admit, I wasn't too keen on doing another one and so we got into an argument: 'Kevin, every player compiles a dream team, it's been done too often before, we should leave it out,' I said.

'Look Dave, I want to do this because there are players that I turned out with and others that I battled against that should be recognised and in any case, I've never seen most of your dream team and as for Dean's biography, whilst he picked some good players, not all of them would be my first choice. Added to which, I was lucky enough to play at three great clubs and against some classy opposition, so I reckon I'm entitled to list my team.'

'Okay Kevin, we'll do it your way,' I said whilst thinking he probably had a point. So for posterity's sake and to avoid Kevin getting angry with me, here is his dream team composed of players he played with along with Kevin's comments:

1. Dale Shearer (Manly)
My Manly team-mate had an electrifying change of pace and caught many world class players napping. He was brave, quick, adaptable and he had a tremendous utility value. He could read a game, he was a tremendous support player with

vision and pace to finish off opponents in the toughest and tightest of situations. His goal kicking ability was the icing on the cake and he played many times for Australia and in the State of Origin.

2. Steve 'Fizzer' Fenton (Castleford)
Like Dale Shearer, Fizzer had exceptional pace but also a devastating side step, I think if he had taken the game a little more seriously, he would have gained international acclaim.

3. John Joyner (Castleford)
John was one of the most amazing runners ever to play rugby; he had bags of pace, poise and vision. These attributes assisted his transition first to off half then loose forward. His 600 plus games is an amazing testimony to his resilience but for me his unselfish approach and his guile and stature put him amongst my Prince of Centres - an easy choice.

4. Michael O'Conner (Manly)
Another superstar centre, he shared many of JJ's qualities with the added bonus of a deft side step off either foot and he too a prolific goal kicker, another who made many State of Origin and full Australian appearances.

5. Alan Hunte (St Helens)
Alan compliments a very explosive three-quarter line. He too had pace to burn, was very competitive and would have scored many tries outside a quality centre like O'Conner.

6. Cliff Lyons (Manly)
A very clever half back with the vision and passing skills to

direct a game. Probably only surpassed by the great Wally Lewis, Cliff was very instrumental in many of Manly's successes and he was also a capable utility player and goal kicker.

7. Bob Beardmore (Castleford)
Much underrated, Bob was exceptionally quick he was also fantastically fit with stamina to spare. We had a tremendous working relationship just as he obviously did with his twin Kevin. He is by a mile the fittest half back I've ever seen.

8. Sam 'Brain' Hughes (Castleford)
All teams have an unsung hero and Sam was just that. Recklessly brave he knew what it meant to put his body on the line. A fearsome one-on-one tackler with hits that belied his stature. Sam was deceptively strong and uncompromising with bags of character.

9. Kevin Beardmore (Castleford)
If he had had a shorter name, I believe he would have made more international appearances as the word is that Frank Myler, the then Great Britain coach, could not fit Beardmore on the back of a cig packet when choosing the team so he chose Brian Noble instead. Kevin and Bob both complimented my style and like his brother he was exceptionally quick with excellent hands. A real class act.

10. George Mann (St Helens)
Deceptively quick for a big guy he also had good off loading skills and his work rate was phenomenal. Like most islanders, he was a fierce and fearless competitor.

11. Keith 'Beefy' England (Castleford)
Another international who in his prime was one of the fittest men I have ever known. Hard, physical and a real competitor, Beefy would top the tackle count and the drives. The tougher it became the more he enjoyed it.

12. Ronnie Gibbs (Manly)
A man of great character and honour he always gave 110 percent. Ron instilled confidence and inspired his teammates with his quick and savage tackling, in fact some of Ronnie's hits were nigh on suicidal. He was respected and feared by all.

13. Mal Reilly (Castleford)
The most influential man on my career. Had Mal led this squad I believe they would have swept any opposition aside. Mal had everything, the skills, the vision and the capability to get the best out of everyone else.

SUBS
14. Shane Cooper (St Helens)
Shane was a New Zealand international and a skilful ball player with the knack to know exactly what to do at the right moment.

15. Gary Connelly (St Helens)
A Great Britain international, Gary is another tremendous utility player and proven try scorer with a solid defence.

16. Des Hasler (Manly)
State of Origin and Australia. As quick as a flash, Des was an aggressive half back and a tough defender.

17. Noel Cleal (Manly)
State of Origin and Australia, a powerhouse block-busting runner who could create havoc when the opposition were tiring.

'So what do you think of my dream team Dave?' Kevin asked after listing his squad.

'It looks pretty good Kevin, but what about adding in the likes of Ellery Hanley, Mal Meninga and Andy Gregory?'

'Yeah, I know what you mean. Ellery was awesome but Mal Reilly just gets my vote because of how he inspired everyone around him. Mal Meninga was probably just as good as John Joyner but I'm picking JJ because he stayed at the top for so long. And as for Andy Gregory, well I guess it's a toss up decision between him and Bob Beardmore, but I'm choosing Bob because he's my mate.'

'Okay Kevin, your dream team it is.'

6

A Worthwhile Adventure

In 1987 when the legendary Mal Reilly first mentioned to Kevin that Manly, the Aussie high flying Silver Tails may be interested in him he was awe-struck. The Sydney competition was universally recognised as the toughest in the world and Kevin was fully aware that although many talented players had preceded him, only a select few had made an impression. Kevin was also aware that Manly was also Mal Reilly's old club where he had performed in the early seventies for several seasons with distinction, so much so that he was held in near legendary regard. Kevin had often heard Mal talk of the beautiful beaches, the laid-back lifestyle, palm fringed seafront walkways and cafe's and bars in abundance. And after talking things through, he drove home from training that very evening eager to confront his wife Margaret with the exciting news. Unsure of her reaction he tossed the pros and cons around in his mind for a while ultimately concluding that he was sure she would be up for it. His speculation proved well founded, Margaret was equally enthusiastic, it was after all the opportunity of a lifetime. Although Kevin was happy at Castleford, he had given his all during a disappointing season and he was convinced that a new playing environment would rekindle his enthusiasm. Mal, whose recommendation had inspired the Manly enquiry, affirmed this.

Victory for Castleford over archrivals Hull in the

Yorkshire Cup Final had been a sweet moment but overall the season had lost impetus on several fronts. St Helens beat Cas in the second round of the John Player Cup and Widnes put them out of the Challenge Cup on an ice rink of a pitch at Wheldon Road. The conditions that day were so bad that had it not been for the fact it was to be televised, there was no way it would have been played. But Widnes adapted better that day to the conditions and Castleford's dreams of retaining the trophy at Wembly were in tatters. It was small consolation to Kevin that Castleford wreaked revenge in a 44-8 league match thumping of Widnes at Wheldon Road. Likewise, with St Helens, victories both home and away 12-10 and 10-8 did not offset not playing in a major final. Then in the league, a late season 16-8 victory over Leeds imbued Cas with confidence for the play-offs. However, Halifax had other ideas and having beaten Cas 9-8 in the Charity Shield at the start of the season they again inflicted disappointment in the play-off with a 16-8 victory. And that despite Cas turning them over home and away in the league!

Mal Reilly was obviously depressed with the ignominious end to Castleford's season and his sense of disappointment pervaded through the team. Added to which, the rumour was that Mal would soon be leaving Cas to take up the full-time GB coaching job, so Kevin and Margaret decided to head for Australia following the adage that a change would be as good as a rest.

Kevin and Margaret stepped off the plane in Sydney, tired, jet lagged and apprehensive of the unknown ahead. Both were eager to taste the prospective lifestyle awaiting, each simultaneously caught sight of the massive sign high above the exit of the arrivals gate: WELCOME TO SYDNEY, it was bold yet sincere Margaret reflected later. Doug Daley the Manly chief executive was in attendance, he recognised Kevin immediately and his warm greeting and quiet gentle mannerisms soon put them both at ease. If either had harboured reservations, these were quickly dispelled. The sight of the bay and Southern Pacific Ocean, its waves washing the sun kissed sandy beach melted their hearts. The flat Manly had allocated them was immaculate, complete with a view of the bay, one side of which was a hub of activity - restaurants, bars and shops and the remainder of the stunning landscape was dotted with expensive looking flats and villas.

Doug Daley didn't stand on ceremony, he briefed Kevin on protocol and what was expected of him then explained the flat belonged to a Welshman who always returned home for six months each Aussie winter. He donated the flat each time to the Manly club for exactly such usage as Kevin and Margaret were to enjoy. The two of them soon settled into the lifestyle, Margaret acquainted herself with the Queens Cliff area and Kevin would jog alternate mornings along Shelly Beach followed by a sea dip to cool off. He was occasionally joined by team-mate Ronnie Gibbs and sometimes by Cliffy Lyons. Both men took a liking to Kevin and helped him settle into this tropical paradise – after all, it was a long way from Bottomboat.

Kevin arrived just after the start of the Aussie season as his team-mates were reaching peak fitness and despite having just concluded a season at Castleford, he freely admits he had to train a damn site harder to meet Manly's standards. When I pointed out to Kevin that he may have been jaded after thirty-odd games with Cas and that the training might just have seemed harder, he responded without hesitation, 'No way Dave, it was more intense with longer sessions. All the players were super fit and unlike home training, it had a much more competitive edge, believe me I found it difficult, I coped and enjoyed it, but the lifestyle and strictness of the regime were a step up from Cas.'

I must confess I felt a bit hurt at these words from Kevin as I had been involved for several seasons at that time with the training programme at Cas and I believed it was a pretty comprehensive set up, in fact I would have backed the Beardmore twins against any Aussie in any aspect of fitness and conditioning. So I asked Kevin why he thought the Manly system had been better.

'Well, a couple of reasons,' he replied. 'First of all the weather is better so you get more continuity with the training because you are outside more, added to which everyone is much more motivated when the sun is shining; much better than running around Pontefract Park when it's pissing down. And second, there was a more professional approach and players didn't go out on the pop so much over there.'

'What, you didn't drink?'

'Now don't get me wrong, I've said before I don't hold with the orange juice culture and the Manly lads were always up for a few beers, it's just that they saved it for after the game rather than mid-week. In any case, you really wouldn't want to face one of their training sessions if you'd had a skinful the night before.'

'What about work Kevin, in England you had a weekday job on a building site which would have helped with your general fitness but did you do anything similar in Australia?'

'Two days a week I had to work with Manly's development officer, coaching the kids in schools, I enjoyed it but soon found it was the club's way of extracting their pound of flesh.'

'I thought you had refused a job offer?' I asked.

'No kidding, that was when we were negotiating my contract. Manly asked me what I did for a living, I answered I work as a labourer on the building sites, so they replied, "Oh we'll be able to fit you in no problem." I told them no bloody way. Wally Lewis didn't work when he came over to Wakefield Trinity, so Kevin Ward isn't about to start labouring in Australia either.'

'Good for you Kevin,' I said.

'But to be fair to Manly, the perks were good, especially our eating-out cards and Margaret and I really made use of them at the Shelly Beach Restaurant owned by an ex-player. We could use our cards for food and only had to pay for drinks, in fact loads of restaurants accepted them.

'From what you're telling me Kevin it seems that an awful lot of money and facilities were invested in the players.'

'There certainly was, at home I might be shovelling concrete eight hours-a-day five days-a-week and then go training. I was hardened and fit, but over there everything was more professional. They had a weights conditioner, sprint coach, general fitness conditioner, gymnastic and flexibility specialist, psychologist, kicking tutor, skills coaches and a media awareness tutor. Everything was planned so that you would be fully prepared for the next game.'

'But a media awareness tutor?'

'Don't forget Dave, rugby league is much more in the spotlight in Australia, much more like football is over here.'

'I'm surprised you haven't mentioned an arse wiper mate.'

'Oh there were some fans willing to do that. But I was so enthusiastic I think I only missed one league match whilst I was over there. I was thirty-two years old but felt like I was twenty-two, it was infectious.'

'Did you want to stay?'

'You bet I did. First day there I called in at Hardboard Diggers, a bar on the sea front and I recognised Jack Baker, a lad from Thorpe who'd been at the same school as me. "Jesus", I said, totally surprised to see a face from the past. Apparently Jack had emigrated nine years earlier, formed his own plastering company and now had an entourage of plasterers downing midis at his expense. The reason I mention Jack is that he said so soon after I arrived, "You won't want to go home Kevin, mark my words," and I didn't and neither did Margaret. Having to come home was a real ball ache and I resented David Poulter refusing my request to stay. I know Doug Daley rang him twice and pleaded on my behalf but all to no avail. Manly had finished the season on a high and they were very confident of reaching the Grand Final to be held for the last time at the Sydney Cricket Ground, it was the chance for a place in history and it looked like I might miss out. In fact I think this was probably the underlying reason why I left Cas a couple of years later.'

'So what was the game like in Australia?'

'It was pretty hard and you had to be prepared to stand up for yourself. One of my first games was against Western Suburbs and they had two crazy props playing opposite us. First time I took the ball, this Bluto look-alike smacked me a beauty and snarled, "Welcome to Australia you pommy bastard". So I picked myself up, played the ball then looked him square in the eye and said, "Fuck you, Alan Parker's slipper hurt more than that". He had a puzzled look on his face - I don't think he understood a word. I took some stick from them both but I gave as good as I got and was still going strong at the end whilst by then they were both sat on the bench covered in a blanket and looking completely dejected. On another occasion, Paul Sironin, totally unprovoked, gave me his best shot. It stung momentarily and I remember the shock on his face when I said, "Is that it, is that your best?" He turned and jogged off sharpish to catch up with play, I don't think he wanted to hang around too long in case I belted him. I think most of the fans expected me to knock seven bells out of him but it wasn't worth it, he knew after that who was the governor and I wasn't going to rise to the bait and get sent off.'

'It sounds like it was pretty intense Kevin.'

'Oh don't get me wrong Dave, it was a bit tougher out on the pitch, especially if you were a pommy, but the whole environment was much more relaxed. I mean, I've seen players like Dale Shearer turn up for a game fifteen minutes before kick off dressed in flip flops and shorts, totally chilled out, but when they walked out on the pitch they were focused and completely ready. I guess that's why I was really sorry to leave and I only cooperated when Manly agreed to fly me back to play in the Grand Final.'

Kevin reported back at Castleford and knuckled down into the opening match against St Helens. He was now being coached by yours truly, and following in the path of Bozo Fulton and Mal Reilly I decided to give Kevin his head. He hadn't been off the plane long but he put himself about and we won 20-10. He then played in three more games where we suffered a shock loss to Leigh away 14-6, then further humiliation a fortnight later at Wigan with a 44-18 drubbing. It had been small consolation that sandwiched in between these two disasters was a convincing Yorkshire Cup first round victory over Hunslet 32-12. Then from the 20th of September, Cas had a ten day break in fixtures before travelling to bitter rivals Featherstone Rovers. For Kevin, this was a vital ten days as he was given leave of absence to fly back to Sydney with Margaret to play in the Grand Final for Manly against Canberra.

Kevin recalls stepping from the plane only to be ushered into an airport anteroom for an unannounced impromptu press conference, Kevin was tired from the long journey but he'd extracted assurances from the club that he would start the match. The press were trying to trip Kevin into divulging something that might cause embarrassment, but he coped with the questions and then the club ferried them across Sydney to the Manly Pacific Hotel.

It was late Monday evening, the build up to the Grand Final was in full swing and the hotel was full to capacity. Reporters and cameramen were constantly slinking about the corridors and foyer looking for scraps, especially anything juicy or controversial. But Bobby Fulton must have decided on a low profile approach, training would be as normal and Kevin reported on the Wednesday for his first session and reintroduction to his team-mates. He was made welcome, he had earned his spurs, he knew his fellow players were glad he was back, the same men were confident that Kev would perform.

Kevin was focused for the rest of the week, yet the approach to the game was so laid back that the players were told to make their own way to the Cricket Ground. Sydney's internationally renowned stadium was about to feature its last ever Grand Final. Players were allowed to turn up at their leisure, some pundits might be aghast at the thought but the score line reflects who got it right. Kevin put all thoughts of jet lag behind him and played a superb game in temperatures of over 100 degrees. And although the match wasn't one of the all-time classics, it was nevertheless admirable rugby given the conditions. In the end, Manly lasted the course better than their opponents and beat Canberra 18-8 to lift the Winfield Cup. All the players suffered in the heat and at the end of the match, Kevin had lost ten and a half pounds in weight, but no matter, he was rightly elated having given his all and come out on the winning side. I asked Kevin about the controversy surrounding the Man of the Match award.

'Well Cliff Lyons won the Clive Churchill Medal and a car. I know lot of fans said I was the best player but I don't know about that, anyway Cliff had a good game and got over for a try so he probably deserved it. In any case I won the Channel Ten best player award and a cash prize of $1,000 and if I had won the car it would have probably cost me a lot more than that to get it back to Cas so I reckon it all worked out okay in the end.'

'So given that very few British players have won an Aussie Grand Final, how did you feel at the end?'

'I'd mixed feelings, I was over the moon that we'd won – for me and the team and all the fans and for my wife and Mal Reilly and Doug Daley, but at the same time I was almost in tears. I was so absolutely knackered that I just wanted to lay down and go to sleep. But then I wanted to celebrate and hold the trophy and party with my team-mates and the fans. I think that's why I felt like crying; there were so many thoughts and feelings going through my head and I was so tired that I was struggling to cope with it all.'

'So what happened then?'

'After a minute or two, I started to get my brain back in

gear and then all the celebrations started. I remember looking at the trophy with the two Aussie players on it and thinking bloody hell, this is a long way from Bottomboat. It was an amazing atmosphere, all the fans were cheering and I think everyone felt a sense of the history as it was the last match played at the Sydney Cricket Ground. Then Mal Reilly came over and shook my hand, he was over there in his new role as Great Britain coach and it was really special to see him because I remembered what he'd said about how he felt when he won a Grand Final. Then after we got changed, the club had arranged for a fleet of white limos to take us back in style with our wives to Manley. When we arrived there, I went looking for Doug Daley to ask if I could stay on a few days to enjoy the celebrations. I found him in the boardroom, near a picture of Mal Reilly, which at the time I thought was very appropriate. I asked Doug if he would speak to David Poulter at Cas and see if I could fly back later than planned. Doug said he would have a word, but later that night he relayed a message from Cas saying, "We have a Yorkshire Cup semifinal on Wednesday and we need you home."

I was touched when Kevin told me this part of his story as I was Castleford's coach at this time and he never put any pressure on me to let him stay on a few days, in fact I didn't even know he'd asked David Poulter and that he had been instructed to return. I had watched the final on TV and I had felt so proud for Kevin but I'm not sure what decision I would have come to had I had personal involvement, maybe I could have had some input with the board, perhaps we could have taken on Featherstone in the semi that Wednesday evening without him, who knows. But there is no doubting Kevin's loyalty and professional attitude because following a post match early morning breakfast reception with his team-mates, he and Margaret bid farewell and boarded the aircraft for the long tedious journey home. Kevin arrived back at Cas and duly turned out in the Yorkshire Cup semi at Featherstone, our carpet-carrying neighbours whom we defeated 36-8, and believe it or not, the most influential player was Kevin Ward, scoring a try and putting Bob Linder over for another. There was no sulking or tantrums from Kevin, he didn't feign any sickness or injuries, he was contracted to Cas and fulfilled his obligations. It's only now when he opens up and tells his story that I realise how important a few more days tasting the sweet success of his labours would have been to him.

As it turned out the Yorkshire Cup proved to be a lucrative occasion for both Bradford and Cas, as a 12-12 draw in the final at Headingley required a replay at Elland Road a fortnight later, so maybe David Poulter's lack of sentiment and instructions to Kevin to fly back immediately proved correct. Anyway, Cas should have won the first encounter, but the team became a little disjointed with the loss of Kevin Beardmore and Bobby Linder who suffered a broken nose courtesy of a frightening clash of heads with his team-mate Johnny Fifita. Then in the dressing room at half-time at Headingley, I recall Kevin offering to move from number ten to hooker. He recognised I needed help and he offered it for the benefit of the team, I respectfully declined, I needed Kevin in a forward position where he was at his most destructive to the opposition and I asked Roy Southernwood to fill the breach. I remember in the post match discussion that we thought we could have taken Bradford and we'd let go an opportunity.

The following week we went to Hull and won convincingly 37-16 and as we approached the replay with Bradford, I believed if Kevin could produce his Grand Final form, we were in with a chance. Confidence was high following the Hull display and Cas were made favourites, but with hindsight I realised we and many others had underestimated Bradford. The second time around we took the field confident. The game was more intense than the first and at the conclusion to a torrid first half, where as always Kevin had led from the front, a brawl started between the two packs. When the hullabaloo died down, the teams headed for the tunnel and then someone started remonstrating with the Cas players in a particularly vociferous way. I turned around and pushed him away, only to then receive a verbal from my own Chairman David Poulter.

'He was the Bradford Chairman,' Kevin laughs. 'I was at the back of you, you did right but I think it was the first nail in your coffin Dave.'

'Well maybe so but when someone is punching you, punch back, when they push, you push back and if they verbalise, well sticks and stones.' Mavis my wife puts two mugs of coffee in front of us both as the laughter subsides. Thinking back I reckon the brawl on the pitch, although honours even, affected our attacking rhythm and we lost 11-2 at the end. It was a dour finish to the Yorkshire Cup campaign. Kevin then put forward, 'Yes and we had to go to Wigan the following week in the first round of the John Player Trophy. You didn't have much luck in draws Sammy.'

'No Kevin, Leeds away in the Challenge Cup later, but I thought we had the beating of Wigan that day if Henderson Gill hadn't pulled off that magnificent tackle on Johnny Fifita late on. I honestly believe we would have won and that would have been some scalp, we suffered the pain without the gain.'

'Well maybe if we didn't gain that day, we did in the following two weeks Dave. Do you remember, I was carrying a thigh injury and we beat Bradford and then Wigan at Wheldon Road?'

'Your memory is better than mine, but I'll tell you something I have researched Kevin, from August 24th 1986 when we played Halifax in the Isle of Man, you played continuous rugby until the 23rd of April 1989, around 120 games in about 128 weeks. Tell me, did you ever feel jaded? Were you ever lacking enthusiasm and did you ever say stuff it, I'm having a steady one today?'

'No mate.'

'A categorical no?'

'A categorical no Dave. To be honest there were times, mainly through injury, when I didn't fancy playing, but invariably up to that point in my career either Mal Reilly or Bozo or you would talk me into having a painkilling injection and stress my importance to the club, the team and myself. So once I ran out of that tunnel I was committed, especially as I believe that at this level anyone can see if you're not giving 100 percent.'

'I never advocated painkilling injections, not then, not now, not ever.' I said.

'What about when I had that cyst on my ankle and it was bothering me?'

'That was Mal who brought the doctor in.' I protested.

'Well you were there.'

I realise that now is not the time to confess that Mal Reilly had asked the doctor to give Kevin an injection to ease the discomfort caused by the cyst, especially as the doctor had said injecting the leg would have little effect. Nevertheless, Mal was adamant. 'Doc,' he said, 'Kevin wants an injection and then he will be happy.' The doctor had replied, 'Okay, I'll inject him with water if it's to be a psychological treatment process.' Mal later beamed as we sat side by side on the bench and Kevin played a blinder.

It was time to conclude our coffee fuelled conversation, Kevin had called at my home from work, it was now 8.00 pm and we had made some progress, some hard yards you might say.

'One last question Kevin before you go. Have you been back to Australia since you retired to relive the old memories?'

Kevin turns his huge frame, totally obscuring any remnants of the late evening light through the open front door. His voice is quiet. 'I daren't risk it with my leg since the injury at St Helens. I went to Cyprus last year, a four-hour flight and my leg blew up twice its normal size. There's no way I could make a long haul flight, I would be at serious risk of thrombosis.'

'What about flying with Garuda Airways, they should rename them Kangaroo Airways, hopping from one stop to another?'

'Yeah, maybe one day.'

7

Big Mack

I had the privilege of playing with Kevin as a ball player forward at both amateur and professional levels. He was a dream to play alongside, something I'm sure such as Barry Johnson the then Cas number 10 will attest. Kevin had a great sense of timing, a robust running back rower, he had the innate skill of judging his run and anticipating the right moment to launch himself, I saw him score many a try with a move close to the opponents' line. Barry Johnson would fill in at half back at the play the ball, he would dummy one way then step out of the grey area in the opposite direction throwing a more outrageous dummy in the guise of feeding another wide runner. He would then deftly slip the ball inside to Kevin who invariably powered over. It was a simple move perfected by practice but the secret of its success was the timing. On this and almost every facet of his game, he was a coach's dream. However, I had an advantage when I coached him, I knew him well, we had a mutual respect and I didn't try to change him. Kevin was a firm believer that if it wasn't broke then don't try to fix it, or even adapt it to a complicated extension. And although I suppose he was set in his ways somewhat when I coached him, that was fine by me as he gave the rock-solid stability that every good team needs. Dependable in attack and defence and yet he possessed another gear; he could and did raise his game another notch when required. But I wondered how Kevin got on at St Helens given that Saints had a reputation for doing things differently and playing with flair, so I asked him about his relationship with the then coach Mike McClennan.

Kevin replied, 'When I signed for Saints Mike said, "I want you to attend training on Thursday night plus Saturday morning and match days initially. When you've got to know all the players and the plays, you can knock out alternate Saturdays." Mike trusted me to keep myself fit, the conditioner would test me every so often which was fine by me, and with that flexibility, the travelling involved from my home in West Yorkshire was minimised. I was happy with Mike, his instructions were simple to follow as were his game plans, if he had a failing at all it was his short fuse, I saw him blow up more than once and pity anyone who crossed him. On one occasion he just about climbed out of a hospitality box window in order to play hell with an irate fan who had been giving him abuse through the glass, believing himself to be in comparative safety. Mike put the fear of God into the poor sod, but luckily he regained his composure before he did anything too drastic. But I reckon I'm fortunate really, I haven't had too many coaches, just Mal Reilly, yourself, Darryl Van de Velde and Mike in this country and Bozo Fulton in Australia. Malcolm was the coach who signed me up as a professional and he was definitely the most influential. As for international coaches, there was Frank Myler, Phil Larder and Maurice Bamford. Maurice was a long time recognising me, but when I made it, I was there to stay. Oh and then there was Graham Lowe for the Rest of the World team against the Aussies, he trained our bollocks off and that was on the back of the 88 tour.'

Of the many times Kevin and myself have met and chatted

hour after hour, even now ten years on, each time the topic might return to his horrific accident his features change dramatically. The pain and suffering is still vivid, he can recall every minor detail, week on week, month on month, with such clarity that I make the point that I wish his memories of his career were equally lucid. I realise that a lot of water has passed under the bridge since he first signed for Cas in November 1978, a handful of A team games and eleven weeks later he was promoted to first team sub. His short spell in the second string under the astute tutelage of the evergreen John Sheridan had erased many of the rough edges in Kevin's game. He learned quickly and his Castleford stats make quite impressive reading. 151 victorious appearances and twelve draws yet during those eleven years, Kevin's outstanding form and consistency was rewarded with a meagre thirteen international caps. I've often speculated that had he played with Saints or Wigan or Leeds throughout the 1980s it would probably have been more. And had he played junior rugby instead of soccer in his formative years, he would no doubt have amassed even more appearances than the 304 plus 12 subs now accredited by the irrepressible historian, Len Garbutt. Kevin was after all twenty-two years old when he signed with Cas, a late starter for sure. His 357 appearances, including spells with Manly in Australia and international matches, well, many would argue it would surely have been higher had he followed the normal accepted route of a junior player. Add in his St Helens stint of 86 matches and 3 sub appearances and we reach a total of 451 - impressive for a late starter! And then when you reckon he only made 18 sub appearances in 14 years, it tells us of Kevin's consistency, reliability and durability because almost 300 of his total games played were at prop, the boiler house stoker, when for many years scrums were competitive and much more physical unlike today.

Part way through this particular meeting with Kevin, a friend of mine 'Big Mack' calls to see me. He greets Kevin warmly and fires the inevitable question, 'So how would you have faired in today's game Kevin?'

'I'm not sure Mack, I would have been fitter as a full-time pro, but who knows.'

I note from Kevin's cautious reply that he holds today's athletes in the utmost respect, however whilst I share Kevin's sentiments I cannot allow Mack to leave without a more forthright answer. 'Mack, Kevin had all the attributes to be even more devastating nowadays than before. He scored eighty-six tries in his career, that's phenomenal for any forward let alone a prop, he was revered at three clubs and holds the distinction of a Wembley winners medal and a Winfield Cup winner, a rare combination held only by an auspicious few. Make no mistake Mack, the Super League era has brought many changes but it hasn't moved so fast since 1993 and if Kevin was turning out this week with either Cas or Saints or whoever, he would be just as sensational as in his heyday.'

'It's a pity we can't turn the clock back,' adds Mack.

Kevin readily concurs yet he is unhesitating in making the point, 'I was lucky, at least my career ending injury was when I was well into my thirties and not earlier.'

'Yes but you were still playing good rugby when you were forced to retire,' says Mack.

'Maybe, but I have to try and keep a positive head on for the sake of Margaret and my son Richard. To be honest, I'm embarrassed when I think back to what they had to put up with. My moods after I broke my leg; I just wanted to get back playing but my leg was just getting worse with one problem after another. I mean I've played in places like New Guinea, New Zealand, France and Australia. The only domestic medal to escape me was a Premiership medal, and then bang, I was out of the game and I couldn't even walk let alone get back into any sort of training and I think the whole thing was just too much of a shock. Up till that time I'd never really considered retiring and then I was instantly on the scrapheap.'

'Yeah, but what a career,' I add.

'That's true, when you persuaded me to turn out for Stanley Rangers that Saturday afternoon, it was the start of a cracking journey. I know I'm luckier than most and it's by remembering that that I've managed to keep my head straight. But I miss the social side of playing and life is much slower than it used to be and I do worry about visiting Cas and St Helens just as an onlooker. I think that would frustrate me even more.'

'Do you still follow the results Kevin?' Big Mack asks.

'Yes, thanks to Sky I watch the games from my armchair and twice a week my appetite is satisfied. Anyhow, it's time I was away.'

'Just before you go Kevin,' Mack asks, 'let me have a look at your leg, I've heard so much about it.'

A slightly embarrassed Kev raises his trouser leg to expose the terrible scars running from above his knee down to his ankle. It's a legacy of what must have been a horrific fracture that nearly resulted in amputation.

8

Reflections

A reflective appraisal of Kevin's career is, I feel, an essential ingredient for the present day reader and fan, many of whom form judgements of a player's prowess by their match statistics.

With fourteen full caps for Great Britain when at Castleford, he stands alongside the admirable John Joyner as the club's joint all-time capped player. John, however, edges in front with two subs appearances. But Kevin went on to match John's stats when with St Helens in 1990 he made two subs appearances against the Kangaroos, and finally edged in front when brought from the wilderness in 1992 to once again face the Aussies and make a career total of fifteen Great Britain appearances plus two at sub.

If Kevin had made the 1984 tour as many expected, he could have added significantly to his total, likewise if he had played most of his career with one of the more fashionable big clubs like Wigan or Leeds, he would no doubt have been selected more often. But Kevin also has two more appearances which for some reason are not recognised by the governing bodies. Firstly, he represented Great Britain against the Rest of the World in the Whitbread Trophy Challenge to mark the opening of the hall of fame in which he scored a try in a 30 points to 28 victory, and was awarded Man of the Match in what the media described as a Herculean display. And second, he was also praised when representing the Rest of the World against Australia in July 1988 in a 22-10 defeat on the back of an arduous tour. Now that tour of 1988, Kevin's only one, seemed doomed before the players embarked on a three-day preliminary trip to Papua New Guinea. For a host of reasons the original squad was decimated and months of preparation work was disrupted, probably more so than on any other tour in history. In Papua New Guinea, Shaun Edwards lasted a mere seven minutes before sustaining an injury culminating in him being sent home for a knee cartilage operation. Then Gary Schofield and Paul Medley were the next on the wounded list, however it didn't end there. Lee Crooks suffered damage to a shoulder, Andy Platt broke his wrist and Paul Dixon soon followed them with a broken thumb, resulting in new men flown in as replacements. The first four games had been victorious but at a devastating cost in personnel. Inevitably the injuries were soon reflected in the performance on the pitch culminating in a sad record breaking three defeats on the trot, the third of which was the first test in Sydney.

When I asked Kevin to comment on this historic one hundredth test match between the two countries he is quick to react. 'We should have bloody won it, Mal had us fired up and we took it to them. We got in their faces and they didn't like it and we were 6-0 up when Ellery scored just before half-time. Then second half Sterlo miscued a kick, it wrong footed our defence and he picked it back up and fed big Sam Backo who scored. It was jammy but they were level. Then even though they scored another, the way we were playing we were still in the game at 12-6.' Kevin heaves a huge sigh before continuing. 'You know Dave, I can remember it like it was yesterday. It doesn't seem like fifteen years ago this week.'

'Go on Kevin, tell me some of the detail.'

'Well Andy Gregory and me had perfected this little run around move and Andy called it on as a gap like the Mersey Tunnel appeared. So I fed him through it and he was in for a try - sweet as a nut. Then that dopey French ref disallowed it for a forward pass, but no way.' Kevin asserts, becoming agitated at this obviously frustrating recollection.

'Did you protest?'

'Yes I called him a Cheating Froggie Bastard. He can't have understood a word 'cos he just smiled, wagged his finger and said, "Forwerd piss, forwerd piss, sorree". I forget his name, Desplot or something.'

'Francois Desplas,' I remind Kevin, 'he reffed you in all three tests.'

'That's right but at 12-12 I think they would have panicked and we would have been lifted. As it was Wally Lewis dropped a goal realising the pressure was on and then a late try by Jackson was when we knew winning was beyond us.'

'But you received the Man of the Match award Kevin, that must have meant something, a consolation perhaps?'

'Maybe now but not then. I was gutted because we as a team had come so close to that historic win. The Man of the Match award could just as easily have gone to Gripper (Kevin Beardmore) or Andy Platt.'

'And the second test Kevin?'

'Best forgotten Dave, Andy Platt broke his wrist, Paul Dixon his thumb, both carried on but we got hammered in the pack that day.'

'So what about the third test? That must have been a bit of an anticlimax with the Ashes lost then Kevin.'

'Not a bit, the third was a World Cup rated fixture, and

anyway we were playing for pride because nobody wants a whitewash to their name.'

'I bet going in to that final match you were the underdogs big style.'

'No kidding, we were a patched up outfit and Mal had to make changes to offset the loss of Gripper, Dixon and Platt. But he got us seriously fired up and we went out looking for revenge and we seriously turned them over. That was a special feeling, the first time in over ten years we had beaten them and our first win on Aussie soil for nearly fifteen years.'

'So then you went to New Zealand needing only a draw to qualify for the World Cup final.'

'Dead right Dave, we thought Desplot the Frenchman had been poor but against the Kiwis we got Mike Stone, a supposedly unbiased ref. Can you imagine, we had just put the fear of God into the Aussies and we get their ref! He disallowed another perfectly good try by Gregs from our run around move and we lost 12-10. We were out of the World Cup Final, I'm sure Stone didn't want the Aussies to take us on. The Aussies then won the final in front of over 47,000 people at Eden Park in new Zealand.'

'So how did you feel about that?'

'Well it had been a hard tour. We were sorry we hadn't made the final and for one reason and another we had to dig bloody deep to get through, but overall it had been great fun and I wouldn't have missed it for the world.'

9

Testing the Water

Kevin answers inevitable questions such as name your most memorable games with the ones that automatically spring to mind, such as the Aussie Grand Final and Wembley 86, but I find there are many more deep down, buried underneath. Careful prompting always seems to bear fruit and when I remind Kevin that he played for Yorkshire in the Old County Championship at loose forward back in 1982, his eyes light up and the flow moves from a trickle to a surge.

'Yes you're right Dave, I remember Kevin Dick was the scrum half, it was at Leigh I think, on a Wednesday night and there were less than 2,000 spectators. We were slow off the mark, Lancashire rattled up twenty-one points before half-time and I remember thinking, "We're going to get stuffed". Terry Flanagan was their loose forward, he played with Oldham and he tore us to ribbons, he threw more dummies in that first forty than they stock in Mothercare. Burkey the Widnes full back kicked goals from all over the park and we seemed to be dead and buried, but it was a game of two halves and we clawed our way back as they started to tire. Kevin Dick went over first then I scored an eighty yarder.'

'How far Kevin?'

'Well it seemed a long way. JJ (John Joyner) got a try in the first half then he put Geoff Pryce from York in for two more in the second. JJ was awesome that day. Kevin Dick kicked a goal off the touchline to make it twenty-one apiece, then the cheeky bugger dropped a goal in the dying minutes and we won 22-21. Bloody hell, that was a good game, I was happy that night but I never got picked again until 1988.'

I take this opportunity to tell Kevin that that was the last ever County Championship on record. 'Oh no wonder I didn't get picked again,' he replies.

Next time it was the War of the Roses series. Yorkshire, Cumbria and Lancashire had performed for eighty-seven years but apathy from the fans made it appear outmoded and Kevin was the last forward to score a try in that historic win - a nice few quiz teasers there.

I carried on the conversation as the big man was warming to my prompting.

'Which game next?' Kevin asked.

I flicked through my notes eager to choose the right one. 'What about your first game against Wakefield Trinity, was that special?'

'Hah it was special all right but for the wrong reasons. We had played Wakefield in a Floodlit Cup match and it was special to me because of my granddad having played for Trinity. I remember the week before I had played at Hull and drawn my first winning pay packet and scored my first try in what was my fifth game. Up till then I had begun to feel I was a jinx because we hadn't won a game when I'd been in the side. Then we beat Trinity the following Wednesday night 22-12 and I was dead chuffed. I had stayed off drinking on Sunday night following the Hull game and Monday because of the Wakefield Cup tie. It was my first professional cup game and a cracking atmosphere under lights. Then after the match I made up for abstaining with a few beers and ended up at Heppy's nightclub in Wakefield. Some of the Wakefield lads were in and we had a good drink, then in a stupid drunken moment, I decided I was capable of driving home, so I turned out of Heppy's car park onto cross Street and left again heading for Wood Street where my car and the police car met nose to nose. Pete Harrision was in the passenger side, I was in a jovial mood and when the copper came out with the "Have we been drinking then?" I came back with the classic, "Only a couple officer". Then he asked me, "Do you realise this is a one-way street?" So I replied, "I'm only going one way." When I think back now, I know it was completely stupid, I don't make any excuses and I guess the smart-arse answers were a combination of drink and trivialising the event to cushion the blow.'

The big man surprises me with this statement, I find it quite profound and somewhat enlightening, it was something of a short, sharp learning curve. No doubt Kevin celebrated many times after that fateful evening but he knuckled down to his rugby and by Christmas 1980 he had featured in thirty-five games, three at loose forward the rest in the second row, scoring eighteen tries, an impressive strike rate for one with so little experience. He recalls his first win at Headingly when he was being mooted as a running robust loose forward. He gave an impressive display in a 34-9 victory that had many knowledgeable peers singing his praises and one prominent pundit likening him to a young Arthur Clues, the prominent Australian forward of the 1940s and 50s.

Castleford in 1980 were at last beginning to make the rugby world take note that they may just be on the verge of a golden era. There was an abundance of young talent coming through the ranks, if they progressed as was expected, then success would prevail. But it was also in 1980 when Kevin tasted the sourness of a big occasion defeat in the John Player Trophy competition. Hard fought wins against Salford away, 15-8 and Widnes at home, 18-10 had earned a semifinal date with Warrington when Kevin reverted to loose forward after playing second row in the previous two rounds. Kevin takes up the story:

'It was a Saturday game at Central Park in December 1980. I finished work on the Friday at lunchtime and all my mates went for a Christmas fuddle while I went straight home. This was my biggest game so far and Warrington were a tough team back then with a good set of forwards and the irrepressible Ken Kelly at the helm. They'd won the trophy twice and been runners up once. Warrington had already won the Lancashire Cup having beaten Wigan a couple of months earlier. Going into the game, we were without two key players; Mal Reilly and damaging runner Geoff Wraith. Mal had been the victim of a cheap Brian Hogan shot in the previous round the week before, which fractured his cheekbone. But typical Mal he was still sending instructions by phone from his hospital bed.'

That Central Park encounter turned out to be every bit as fierce as the previous week with stalemate at the end of eighty bruising minutes. Kevin relates that he was impressed by the pace of the Warrington back rowers Martyn, Eccles and Hunter. 'They were like gazelles,' he mused briefly adopting a pose of the thinker, 'and that winger, big bugger he was, what was his name Sammy?'

'Well they were both big but I think you mean Hesford.'

'Yes, Steve Hesford, he could kick goals from anywhere, oh it's all coming back to me now. Dave Finch kicked a late goal and we drew 5-5, I thought we were the best side. Shag (John Sheridan) standing in for Mal said we should tackle them out of the game and we did. The replay was at Headingly the following Sunday but we had to play Wakefield away on Boxing Day first. We beat Wakey 23-8, that was the Friday, Saturday was a rest day, then we took them on and we lost. I can't remember the score but I do know Ken Kelly had a field day, he played us off the park.'

I remind Kevin that my research shows it was 22-10 and that Warrington went on to win the final against a plucky Barrow side. Kelly capped an impressive first season as club captain winning the Truemans Man of Steel award and the divisions Players Player of the Year. Ex St Helens centre Billy Benyon, who was then with Warrington, was the Coach of the Year, a fair reward for his brave approach in blooding so many young Warrington based lads. There would be many more fierce encounters between Cas and Wires in the ensuring years, yet Cas had chances to secure the win in that five all draw. Later that season Castleford once again considered themselves unlucky to lose in the second round of the Challenge Cup, going down narrowly at Widnes, seven points to five. The Cas team complained bitterly as with only forty seconds remaining Kevin was penalised for being offside under his own sticks. John Myler took advantage and kicked that all-important goal. 'Hey Kevin, I'd forgotten about that one, were you offside?'

'I've never been offside in my bloody life!'

'History says you were that day, a lesson learned I guess.'

This loss must have injected a little steel into this young Cas side because they went on to record five wins from seven games to finish a respectable fifth place in the table, which on occasions they had topped that year. A trip to Wakefield was the reward in the Premiership play-offs and a comfortable 25-8 win set up a semifinal date with archrivals, the Knocker Norton inspired Airle Birds. Now if the heartbreak of being nearly men during this season gone was lying heavy on the minds of the Cas lads, it didn't show one bit. They played their hearts out, they played with confidence too, but it was all in vain losing by the narrowest of margins, 12-11. A season of so near yet so far, some of the Cas youngsters were still developing, many had faced heartbreak several times and time would tell if they were to continue to develop both individually and as a team.

Kevin and his team-mates, Gary Hyde and Steve Fizzer Fenton, had been recognised by the powers that be that they were players for the future. All three had featured in the last three consecutive Under 24 internationals; in fact, Kevin played his first representative game after only eighteen first team appearances. It was on the 13th of January 1980 against France in Carcassone, and many of those players that day went on to become household names following their 11-7 victory. The team was: 1. Mick Burke (Widnes), 2. Des Drummond (Leigh), 3. David Stephenson (Salford), 4. Mike Smith (Hull KR), 5. Steve Fenton (Cas), 6. Ian Rudd (Workington), 7. Neil Holding (St Helens), 8. Roy Holdstock (Hull KR), 9. Paul O'Neil (Salford), 10. Keith Rayne (Wakefield), 11. Kevin Ward (Cas), 12. Kevin James (Bramley), 13. Harry Pinner (St Helens), 14. Steve Dennison (Hull), 15. Alan Rathbone (Leigh), Coach: Johnny Whiteley (Hull).

After a while, our conversation, as so often before, moves onto different things. We are never short of material to discuss and I have access to his career details from my research and my own memory. Added to which, we both keep in touch with the modern day game, I often watch matches at Wheldon Road and follow my local team, Stanley Rangers, and Kevin, although not so keen to return to the stadiums, reads the rugby press and tunes in to the games on TV. Apart from our obvious interest and enjoyment, it keeps us abreast of topical items, which we are able to debate. No item commands a lengthy discussion, Kevin is a good listener but when he has made his appraisals, proffered his analysis and concluded with his viewpoint, I am quick to realise if I disagree I'll not change him. His personality, and he has plenty, is demonstrated in the style he played the game, direct, forthright and consistent. And during many of these debates Kevin will utter comments such as 'no-way', 'whatever' or 'I don't think so' in a manner which makes it obvious that the particular subject is closed. He never stood on ceremony as a player and I guess it's nice to see he hasn't changed in that respect, although he has mellowed like most would expect of a forty-seven year old and he does, despite his leg injury, appear totally content and at peace with the world. I never try to be patronising to Kevin, we have come a long way since his youth when he perhaps perceived me as something akin to his school teacher, after all I was landlord in one of his often frequented pubs at that time, then later his coach at Cas, plus he worked alongside my brother in our building business for several years. Yet our relationship has always been one of friendship and admiration. I am fully aware that through sheer determination and an iron will to succeed, he rightly scaled the pinnacles of rugby league, so when we speak to each other, it's with mutual respect. I tap into his reservoir of thoughts for the benefit of this story and the reader and whilst doing so, I feel very privileged indeed.

To a certain extent, I am capable of controlling the ebb and flow of Kevin's recollections. If I mention coaches, his back straightens like a rod, if I bring up his old school years he relaxes and a big smile breaks across his features, if I mention his wife Margaret and Richard his son, he speaks warm and endearingly and if I mention the modern game he responds with zestful enthusiasm. I suspect he lacks the opportunity these days to have meaningful conversations with his equals, this enthusiasm endorses to me at least, that such as Kevin and many like him, could offer an input into the direction that the modern game of rugby league is heading. I strongly refute the claim that dinosaurs of yesteryear are best buried by time. Kevin is no dinosaur, although Alex Murphy christened him Barney Rubble from the Flintstones in the eighties during his TV summarising. But the St Helens players rightly recognised he was a leader and endearingly re nick-named him Fred. But to hear Kevin break down some of the finer points of the modern game gives cause for alarm as it is endorsed by his refreshing honesty. Kevin points out that he has noticed a growing cynicism creeping into the game, cynical methods of tackling coached into teams by cynical coaches determined to inflict maximum damage on a fellow player. 'I'm all ears on this one,' I say as he enlightens me with his view on something that I had only heard vague rumblings of in the press. Kevin points out that in a recent match, Huddersfield made a multiple tackle where they were deliberately attempting to manoeuvre the ball carrier into a vulnerable position to complete the tackle with maximum damage to his limbs or torso. He continues, 'The gang tackle of my time was outlawed by the rugby league, now we're seeing something similar where two players deliberately hold up the tackled player for say two seconds, a third player enters the tackle and they then drive the opposition player into the ground.

Then to add insult to injury, they climb off the player slowly, one after the other, so as not to upset the ref. It's all designed to slow the play the ball and it's bloody cynical.'

'I'll take note next time I watch Huddersfield Kevin.'

'It's not just Huddersfield, there are other teams playing the same tactics as a damage limitation exercise, it must be being coached because it is so systematic and so cynical.'

'So what do you suggest?'

'It's up to the ref to be quicker and call "held, release him"; he's in charge so he has to lay down the law.'

'Eh Kevin that would catch the defensive line in no man's land!'

'Yeah English administered justice meted out on the biologists who are spoiling the game.'

'What do you mean biologists?' I ask, confused.

'Well they dissect every aspect of the game as though they are cutting open a rat in a laboratory.'

'Isn't that thorough coaching, just trying to find an advantage?'

'Yes if it's within the rules. Look Dave, the spirit of the game is fast going out of the window, take players wearing padding.'

'Yes?'

'Well they can only wear it for protection, nothing can be worn that will inflict damage right.'

'Okay, I'll agree.'

'So you can't use artificial aids to give you an advantage.'

'No.'

'Then why can a kicker like Brandan Costin come to kick a ball from the half way line with the aid of a foot high cone?'

'But the cone's not inflicting damage Kev.'

'Dave the ball is in the air so long, the spectators have

dozed off and the chasing tacklers are on the receiver before he gets a head of steam, it's an unfair advantage, the receiver gets smashed and the non offending side are pinned on their own line and all caused by a cone.'

'Okay, maybe you have a point, so what's the answer to that one, some sand?'

'No don't be daft; it just needs a standardised cone provided by the ref or touch judge, a cone that is the same for all.'

'I think maybe you are a biologist yourself Kevin!'

'Bollocks Sammy, I'm serious.'

At that moment I decide Kevin has given his usual indication to change the subject but when I later reflect on the discussion, I have to agree it's a cynical way to restart a game and maybe he does have a point

'Shall we go for a pint mate?'

'Just one I'm driving.'

A teenage night out with the lads.

Total concentration at an early age.

Picture, Sig Kasatkin

A formidable trio; Kevin Ward, Kevin Beardmore and Barry Johnson.
Picture, Sig Kasatkin

Chairman David Poulter introduces the Castleford front three to Princess Alexandra before the 1986 Challenge Cup final at Wembley.

Wembley 1986, pre-match acknowledgement to the Castleford fans.

Two Stanley Rangers, Kevin Ward and Gary Lord, celebrate in the bath after Castleford's Challenge Cup triumph over Hull KR.

The team embark on their 1986 Challenge Cup victory parade in the traditional open topped bus.

The Castleford fans crowd in to celebrate with their victorious heroes.

Nicky Kiss clears the ruck with Kevin and Johnny Fifita as markers.
Picture, Sig Kasatkin

It was never a penalty!

Picture, Sig Kasatkin

Kevin proudly sports his coveted Great Britain jersey.

Picture, Sig Kasatkin

Canberra's Chris O'Sullivan bravely faces up to a charging Kevin Ward in the 1987 Grand Final at the Sydney Cricket Ground.

Picture, News Ltd

Champagne mood, champagne occasion, Grand Final success with Manly.
Picture, News Ltd

Great Britain V France 1988. Kevin keeps up the pressure in a 30-12 victory at Headingley.

Picture, Sig Kasatkin

Kevin in action...

Drop off pass.
Picture, Sig Kasatkin

Hitting the line.
Picture, Sig Kasatkin

Making the ball available.
Picture, Sig Kasatkin

Change of direction at pace.
Picture, Sig Kasatkin

...demonstrating his skills.

Offloading under pressure.
Picture, Sig Kasatkin

Bursting through the defensive line.
Picture, Sig Kasatkin

Catching on the burst.
Picture, Sig Kasatkin

Attentive marking.
Picture, Sig Kasatkin

Inseparable club and international team-mates, Kevin Beardmore and Kevin Ward on Great Britain duty.

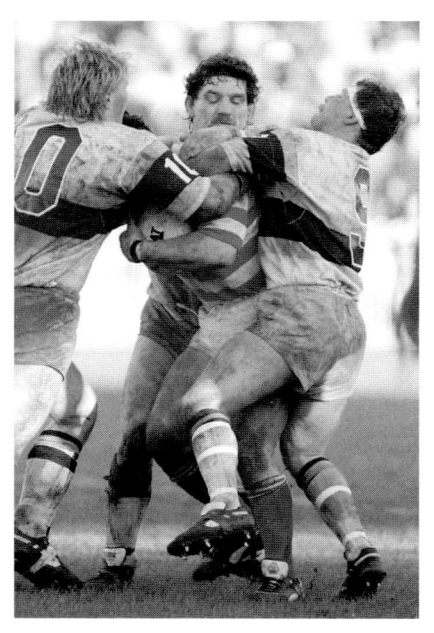

Picture, Sig Kasatkin

Nowhere to go! Dean Sampson, Kevin Ward and Kevin Beardmore.

Picture, Sig Kasatkin

Great Britain versus the Rest of the World. Despite attention from Noel 'Crusher' Cleal and Kurt Sorensen, Kevin scores a vital try.

Picture, Sig Kasatkin

Come on, drink up. Kevin and Margaret enjoy a night out.

A brief stint under Darryl Van de Velde. Castleford 1989-90 pre-season photograph.

Picture, Sig Kasatkin

Oh no – not Wigan again!

Picture, Sig Kasatkin

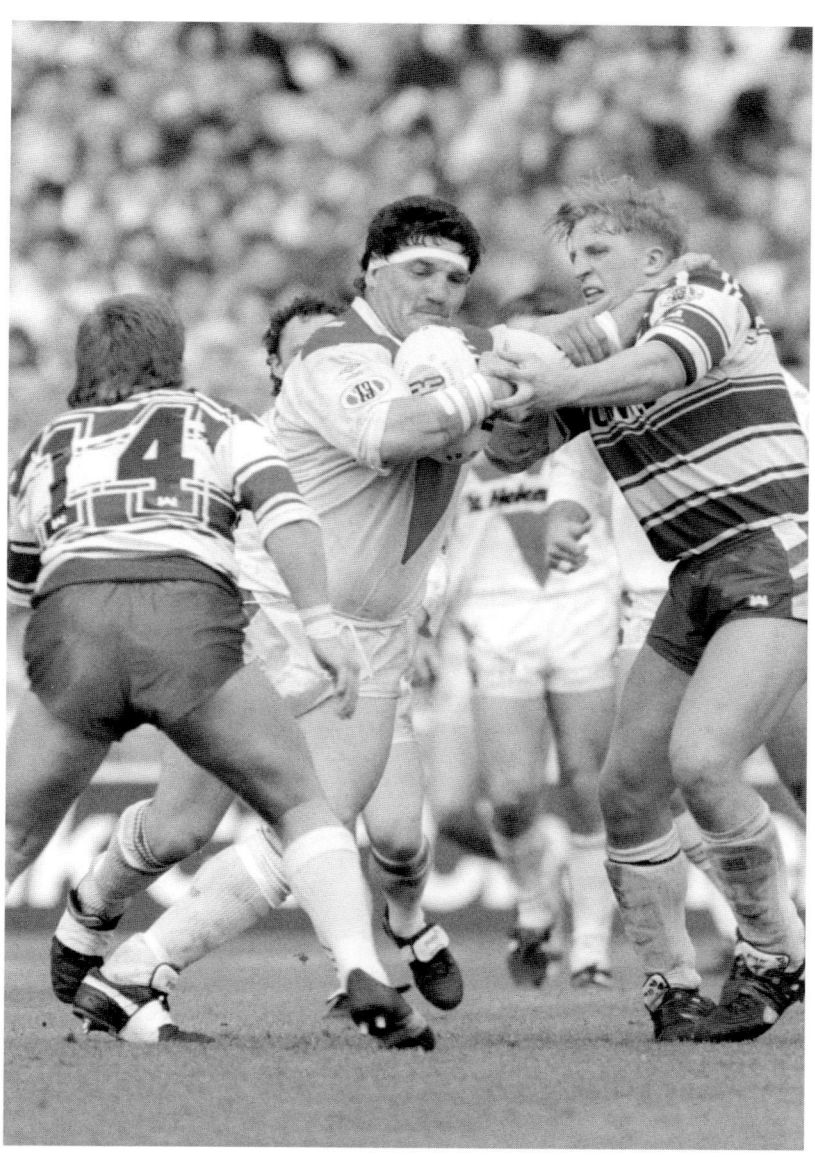

Kevin on the surge for Saints as Wigan try to tackle.

Picture, Sig Kasatkin

Karl Fairbank and Kevin Ward on the Great Britain bench in the 19-12 victory over Australia at Wembley, October 1990.

Picture, Sig Kasatkin

Gimme the ball. Kevin in support.

Picture, Sig Kasatkin

Saints celebrate winning the Lancashire Cup 24-14 over Rochdale Hornets.
Picture, Sig Kasatkin

Making the hard yards.
Picture, Sig Kasatkin

St Helens celebrate with the Charity Shield after their 17-0 victory over Wigan at Gateshead.
Picture, Sig Kasatkin

Kevin and Margaret with a young Richard.

Kevin rides a tackle in another Saints V Wigan derby.

Picture, Sig Kasatkin

Dressed to kill! Great Britain team-mates Kelvin Skerrett and Kevin Ward, normally bitter rivals, make pre-match assessments.

Picture, Sig Kasatkin

Dad and son enjoying a holiday

Johnny Got It Wrong. Andy Platt, Martin Dermott and Kevin Ward stand for the national anthems before the 1992 World Cup Final against Australia at Wembley.

Picture, Sig Kasatkin

And the nurse said no more than two visitors round a bed. Kevin undergoing treatment on his broken leg.

Kevin's testimonial, St Helens V Castleford at Knowsley Road and a farewell to both teams fans.

10

Learning How to Win

Kevin's first cup final as a professional sportsman was against Bradford Northern on Saturday the 3rd of October 1981, the event; the Websters sponsored Yorkshire Cup Final. A disappointing crowd of only 5,852 graced Headingley with their presence, those who stayed away made a wise decision. A drab dour game ensued, only occasionally brought to life by the deft touches of a young Barry Johnson and the inspirational leadership of John Joyner who had taken over as Captain from the injured Mal Reilly. Kevin partnered the speedy David Finch in the second row and together with the young Andy Timson at loose forward, they proved equal to the task of matching Northern's formidable back three of Idle, Van Bellen and Rathbone. Castleford deservedly won the game with two tries to one, the first of which a JJ pass put the irrepressible George Claughton through the narrowest of gaps. He strode majestically out of Mumby's attempted tackle and handed on to the supporting Gary Hyde who finished unopposed. But the half-time score of 5-2 was indicative of the games dourness, although to be fair to Cas, Mal Reilly duly pointed out to his charges that Bob Beardmore and Steve Fizzer Fenton could have scored had they had a little more composure. Bob must have taken Mal's words to heart in the early part of the second half when he performed a simple yet effective run around with the ever-skilful Barry Johnson. He then fed John Joyner playing in the unaccustomed stand off position, John sprinted clear to touch down and apart from a further Bradford try to Alan Parker, a late Bradford revival was contained and 10-5 at the end meant a first winners medal for Kevin and one which he treasures dearly to this day.

When prompted he briefly reflected; 'It was hard-earned, it may not have been pretty to watch, but defensively Bradford at that time were very strong. Hanley and Redfearn could tackle like forwards and Graham Idle and Rathbone never knew when to give in, they would still be tackling now if the ref hadn't blown for time, yes it was a tough game that one!'

'Looking at the records Kevin your league campaign was woeful that year, any reason spring to mind?'

'Hell Dave I can't remember that far back, oh except for the cup run, I had set my sights on Wembley.'

'So had Hull, Kevin.'

'Hmm, they were our bogey team that year, they beat us four times, twice in the league and in the third round of the John Player Trophy which they went on to win if my memory serves me right.'

'Yes Kevin, Hull beat Hull KR twelve to four.'

'We were still confident going into that semi that we were good enough to win even though we had several players injured, but we lost 15-11. That was a hard game and it hurt like hell, losing by four points was the end of our season, literally. It had a bad effect on most of the players and we only won a couple more games.'

'Didn't Hull go on to win the Challenge Cup?'

'Yes against Widnes, they drew at Wembley and won the replay at Elland Road. Some great players on view in both teams.'

'So a damp squib conclusion, no play-offs, nothing.'

'Well Yorkshire Cup winners and Challenge Cup semifinalists was I suppose some consolation, but I think from a personal point of view, it was the last game of the season up at Barrow when Mal picked me for the first time at prop, that was my most significant memory. He suggested my future might be there long term. Trevor Skerrett at Hull had made a similar move in the Wembley game against Widnes. That Summer I really picked up on my weights programme, increasing my upper body strength and bulk. I was aware this would restrict my mobility and could slow my pace but the idea of moving to prop appealed to me. In the game at that time there were some good hard-running back rowers such as the Gorley brothers, the up and coming Lee Crooks, Eric Prescott, Mike O'Neal, John Fieldhouse, Andy Goodway, Mick Worrell, the Rayne twins, the list was endless. Mal and me reckoned that many of the good props were ageing fast, so my opportunity for honours would be enhanced by moving up front.'

'Well history proved it worked Kevin.'

'Maybe so, but it was a long time coming. Half of those players I mentioned also moved up to prop, anyway as it turned out the following season, out of twenty-eight played I made only twelve starts at number eight, so I suppose my transition to prop was gradual rather than sudden.'

'Ah yes, the eighty-two eighty-three season, any significant events during that period?'

'Well I started in the second row for the first four games, then the twelve games at prop were consecutive, so I believed at the time I was established and I had scored five tries so I deemed that a bonus.'

'Did the team do well?'

'Not too badly in the league, up to Christmas we won eight from eleven, a big improvement on the season before.'

'And in the cups?'

'Bloody disaster. We got walloped 33-10 at home to Leeds in the Yorkshire Cup and lost 16-10 to Wigan in the JPS Cup and to boot, in January 1983 I was back in the second row. A couple of weeks later we were back on the Challenge Cup trail determined to go one better than the previous year. Even when we were drawn at Wigan. We were not fazed, we beat them 17-7 and confidence was sky high. Then we beat Barrow 14-9 away, followed by a resurgent Hunslet at Elland Road 13-8 and two weeks later we were back at Elland Road for the semifinal.'

'Need I ask who you were playing Kevin?'

'No you don't, it was Hull again. We were so determined it was scary, the odds were on our side, the law of averages and all that.'

'I can vaguely recall most of the match Kevin but the Jimmy Leulai try for Hull near the end was a piece of magic that vividly springs to mind. He broke from halfway, stepped first left then right and scored without a hand being laid on him.'

'Trust you to remind me of the details Dave.'

Once again, Cas had failed to lay aside the hoodoo and Hull went to Wembley to face Featherstone, where it is well documented history that the Colliers achieved where the Glassblowers failed, taking the trophy back to Post Office Road after a 14-12 victory. Two days after the semifinal, Cas again faced Hull and managed to overcome them 21-16, Kevin scoring a vital try. Four wins on the trot following that semifinal defeat earned Cas a Premiership play-off place and the reward of a daunting trip to Hull Kingston Rovers but Cas lost 14-35. The team was being fast-tagged under achievers, so the search for consistency continued and the rigours of pre-season training was soon upon them. Kevin put in another power packed weights programme, bitterly disappointed at missing a coveted Wembley appearance yet again.

During the run up to the 1984 summer tour, after being overlooked for the Great Britain team to take on the French side in Avignon, when David Hobbs and Mick Worrell were preferred, Kevin was selected for the return fixture at Headingley in the unaccustomed position of number ten. Although he had gained a little experience of propping at number eight, it was only about a dozen matches to date in his career, he was still at that time predominantly a second rower. However to be honoured with your first full cap so close to home was enough for Kevin and he started at number 10 for Cas in the first round of the Challenge Cup at Kent Invicta on February 11th, six days later.

The match against France was a dour, uninspiring event, Great Britain winning 10-0. No one had particularly shone in either game and did little to enhance their tour prospects, least of all Kevin. The press were scathing, airing the view that Kevin had been hugely disappointing which seems unfair given his lack of experience in the position, never mind that it was his first cap. But the bad publicity seemed to stick and Kevin wasn't selected for the tour.

When I asked Kevin to reflect, he stated, 'I don't think I played badly, I didn't knock on or lose the ball, I did my tackling and heaved the ball forward hard and often and the French tackled particularly well as they had done in the previous game.' His face saddens as he continues, 'I was really upset not to tour and disillusioned but Mal Reilly had a word with me and said he was giving me an extended run at number eight. He consoled me that when touring teams are picked, some unjustifiable selections are made and that it was unfortunate I wasn't selected, especially as my club form had earned me my GB call up. Mal said he thought the selectors had got it wrong and that they were probably influenced by politics and favouritism.'

As things turned out, the Great Britain loss turned out to be Castleford's gain and true to Mal's word, Kevin played at number eight, culminating in the Premiership final at Headingley against Hull KR. It was Kevin's thirteenth game on the trot, ten of which were won since that fateful international. I remind Kevin of a newspaper article that stated he gave an inspired performance that day, even though Roger Millward, their wily coach had started with three props to nullify the mighty charges of Kevin and fellow prop Gary Connell. Kevin adds, 'Crafty bugger was Roger we were 8-0 up at half-time although it should have been more and we knew it. Roger took Millington, one of the props off at half-time and switched Mike Smith to the pack. Him and Dorahy cut us up a bit and we lost 18-10.'

Many pundits explained away Castleford's loss to an epic performance the previous week against an inform Hull team which had taken its toll on some of the players. In beating Hull, Cas had turned four previous defeats during that season alone into a magnificent 22-12 semifinal win. The Hull bogey had finally been demolished only to be reinvented by their east of the town neighbours. The Harry Sunderland Trophy was deservedly won by John Dorahy but accounts say he was run close by Kevin Ward.

The tourists returned without a test win, yet several young players had done their emerging reputations no harm. Noble, Hanley, Drummond and Schofield, were all approached by Aussie clubs. Kevin believes that had he been in the shop window he too would have made an impact.

Two of Kevin's team-mates who did tour, Kev Beardmore and John Joyner, whilst only making a test appearance each from the subs bench on the New Zealand leg, they had nonetheless returned home super fit, probably thanks to a good attitude and the efforts of Rod McKenzie, the conditioner. Cas and Kevin were full of optimism at the commencement of the 1985 season but it turned out to be misplaced. The two overseas signings were pedestrian in comparison with previous years. A first round exit from the Yorkshire Cup at home to Leeds 14-16, an ignominious second round exit in the John Player Trophy away at Halifax 20-16 and only six wins from the first eighteen games. It took eight wins from the next ten games, including three in the Challenge Cup, to put a smile back on the faces of fans, players and the coaching staff. As they approached the semifinal of the Challenge Cup against, you guessed it, Hull, at Headingley on the 6th of April, questions were again asked whether Cas would once more stumble in a cup match against the Airlie Birds. Cas had beaten them in the league two weeks earlier 26-18 at Wheldon Road. The game had been a thriller but in a big game like the Challenge Cup semi, Hull's star packed side would be a giant task. Hull had a wealth of overseas internationals to draw on including Jimmy Leulai, Fred Ah Kuoi, Gary Kemble, Dane O'Hara and John Muggleton, plus the cream of young British Talent with Lee Crooks, Steve Norton, Paul Rose, Trevor Skerrett and Gary Schofield thrown in. And with others such as Steve

Evans and Gary Divorty, it was an ominous task for Castleford. This season to date, Hull had won the Yorkshire Cup and were runners up to their equally star-studded neighbours Hull KR by twelve points to nil in the John Player Trophy final. So quite rightly, Cas were the underdogs. They had no chance of making the play-offs in the league so this semi was to be the last chance saloon, the one game that could resurrect their season. Mal Reilly called on all his expertise, quietly reminding players of their responsibilities and subtly trying to ease the tension. A crowd of over 20,000 dominated by a sea of Black and White greeted the teams at Elland Road with the resonating sound of Old Faithful. Cas fans, although less in numbers, were equally vociferous hoping that it was their day, their time, after all it was Castleford's third Challenge Cup semifinal in four years, even the law of averages was surely on their side.

Kevin recalls that it was a tough first twenty minutes.

'I know,' I reply, 'I was on the bench as Mal's assistant.'

'Oh yes, I forgot.'

The deadlock was broken on twenty-one minutes with a Dane O'Hara try yet it was too far out to goal. Cas fought back and were rewarded with a classic from John Joyner and then another from Gary Hyde. At 10-4 with not long remaining, Hull's Peter Sterling hoisted a high ball and John Muggleton scored from it.

'That was a sickener,' Kevin comments, 'we were camped on the Hull line for the last five minutes; a drop goal would have been enough.' A sigh then silence, even now twenty years on you can taste the tension during those moments.

The replay was scheduled for the following week giving just four days to rest those weary limbs. However both teams had a Slalom League fixture to fulfil on the 8th, so Mal Reilly asked me to field the whole A team. We did and against a strong Halifax side we went down 20-30. It was a valiant performance by the Cas youngsters and only late in the game when Halifax were 20-18 down when they broke. But then it was time to again engage the old enemy for the ultimate prize. This time the fans were rewarded with an awesome game, often recalled as one of the best Challenge Cup ties ever. It had everything, tries of the highest quality, nail biting tension, an all-in brawl, Gary Kemble carried off and Ian Orum reprimanded. Lee Crooks was probably the difference between the two teams and he landed three vital goals, the actual winning margin of six points in Hull's 22-16 victory.

To be beaten in a semi is tough; to be beaten in a replayed one is heartbreaking and Castleford were now becoming known as the nearly men. Kevin's only consolation at this time was that he had been in tremendous form, equally at home in the second row or at prop. But the season closed with a whimper and Cas in twelfth place so the club's playing and coaching personnel simply rolled up their sleeves and prepared. They embarked on a close season tortuous training programme that bordered on masochistic. As Kevin hauled his ever-broadening shoulders to new heights of attainment in the weights room, his fellow players responded. Kevin was the yardstick with the weights but when it came to the interval running, Kev Beardmore and brother Bob set the lead along with Dave Rookley over the hills of the Kippax and the track of Pontefract Park. John Joyner, Tony Marchant, Dave Plange and Gary Hyde honed their speed with inspired sprint drills, so competitive that sickness invariably followed. Legs would weary and tremble with fatigue as the blood craved for more oxygen to replenish drained cells. Then to finish, 300-metre relay sprints, repeated four times with a five-minute recovery period. I well remember Kevin Beardmore saying, 'We might not be the best team in this league but we must be the fittest.' Something was simmering; the feel good factor was blatantly in our faces. A fit squad is a happy squad, a happy squad is a confident squad, a confident squad will be a winning squad. All this had been fuelled on the back of that replay defeat.

Unlike the previous season which opened with four losses, Cas were quick off the blocks and a hard fought, yet rare win at Wigan, was followed up with four more on the trot against Sheffield, Hull, Hunslet and York. Warrington upset the applecart by inflicting a 24-16 defeat but Cas bounced back to record three more wins over Halifax, Swinton and Leeds; the latter a Yorkshire Cup semifinal win at Headingley. Cas were averaging over twenty-seven points per game and conceding only ten but two more losses split by a win against St Helens dented these figures. However Cas were back in a final, the Yorkshire Cup against the mighty Hull KR, holders of the John Player Trophy, beaten finalists in this cup and First Division champions the season before.

Kevin takes up the story, 'Hull KR were more tactically aware at that time and that was their single biggest asset. A Roger Millward coached John Dorahy with Gavin Miller directing traffic.'

'They were like cats with mice then Kevin,' I add.

'No mate, we were never mice, no I mean in the way they patiently stalked you then they would strike.'

'Oh more hunters then.'

'Yes exactly, mind you Dave, that win at Leeds was something to be remembered.'

'I remember Kev, Mal took you and the rest of the pack off to one side before the game and gave you a private audience.'

'Yes mate, he was fed up of coming second, he demanded we laid the platform for a win and then we watched that video in the dressing room.'

'Yes I chose that Kev. I showed it to Mal, he gave it the green light and Johnnie Walker set up the TV and video for me, what a man he was Kevin.'

'Yeah, one of the good guys.' Kevin states melancholically. 'Yes I remember on the video Barry McGuigan before his fight with Pedroza, his dad sang Danny Boy in the ring. The look in Barry's eyes said it all, he was so proud of his dad, nothing was going to stop him winning that world title that night.'

'That was the idea, it was meant to inspire you.'

'I remember we kicked off to Leeds long and high, and the chase was so good that when we met Brendon Hill driving the ball out, we picked him up and carried him back ten metres into the in goal. That first thirty seconds were the platform for that win, believe me Dave.'

'I do Kev I was there.'

Kevin then adds, 'Leeds had won six on the trot when we turned them over, so the cup final against Hull KR was a bit of an anticlimax.'

'I don't know about that Kevin, if I remember rightly, the Robins had notched up a 22-6 lead by the hour but then those powerhouse surges of you and the other forwards started to tell and you drove Hull KR onto the back foot. If my memory is correct, Tony Marchant was held up over the line on sixty minutes but then due to your driving runs he scored two tries and with about five minutes to go we were hovering on triumph.'

'That's true but Hull KR held on.'

'They did and the Man of the Match award, went to John Dorahy, his clinical kicking equalled the record of five in a Yorkshire Cup final, he was a worthy winner.'

It had been so near yet so far once again for Cas. Kevin's only consolation was that the press had seemingly been won over and they praised his display throughout. He was gradually creating an impression of invincibility, his now awesome power and superb conditioning was, together with more experience, making him the most talked about forward in Britain.

11

Laying the Ghost to Rest

On the international front Kevin's disappointment at being omitted from the Frank Myler coached 1984 tour party saddened many people, Mal and myself were particularly gutted for him. We were aware of the hard work Kevin had put in on all aspects of his game added to which his form had been outstanding, so being called into the squad to train merely raised false hopes. Wayne Proctor from Hull was drafted in for whatever reasons, but at the time, it was suspected that with Dick Gemmell as tour manager, there was no need to look any further for answers why. However when the coaching regime was changed and Maurice Bamford took the helm with Phil Larder as his assistant, Kevin was more optimistic that his chance was not too far away.

1985 was the year of the Kiwi tour to Britain and Kevin's early season form had been awesome, especially in defeat to Hull KR in the Yorkshire Cup final. Kevin recalls, 'I was frustrated, it seemed that anybody and everybody could wear one of the new styled international jerseys but me.' A disgruntled Kevin was akin to an angry Rhino, his charges became more ferocious as he drained the dregs of his emotions to once again prove an international place had to be found for him, even though he couldn't establish a place with Yorkshire. By the end of 1985 Kevin had one Yorkshire, three Under 24s and one full international to his credits, which was scant reward for six seasons of consistently outplaying some of the more favoured names. All coaches have preferences since time immemorial, club coaches elevated to rep coach or national coach would have an input into selection and it was equally fair to assume that their preference for a playmaker and a pack leader be one or two of their own club men. And to some extent it made sense, some long-standing relationships proved successful at both levels, take for instance Peter Fox, Deryck Fox and Jeff Grayshon with Bradford and of course Maurice Bamford was in many ways cloned with Peter. But he was justified in his selections that year with two victories, two draws and just one defeat. His bold selection of John Fieldhouse at number ten was repaid with John walking away with the Man of the Series against New Zealand. Lee Crooks plus the old warhorse Jeff Grayshon had also acquitted themselves well and things just did not auger well for Kevin. Thankfully the Wembley Cup Final win eased the seasons despair on the international front, as did the news just prior to Wembley that Bamford had chosen him in the twenty-nine man squad to face the Aussies in the autumn. Had Kevin finally convinced the authorities that it was his time? History shows he had. Of the next fifteen international matches Kevin Ward was to feature in thirteen of them, eight with his club team-mate Kevin Beardmore.

Back at Cas confidence had been dented for some inexplicable reason, a first round JPS match loss away to York 12-10 further deepened the gloom that had descended over Wheldon Road, only briefly lifted with two wins from ten games. Kevin recalls it well. 'We were fit and we were trying but we were not getting the results and self doubt was beginning to creep into the camp. Then we got stuffed at Hull the week before the Challenge Cup first round at Hunslet and Mal read the riot act. We were probably, as was suggested, feeling sorry for ourselves. I think we had begun to believe the "perennial bridesmaids" tag that the press had given us. Then the Challenge Cup came at just the right time. First we had Hunslet away and a sixty points to six win put fire in our bellies. It was sweet and just what we needed. Ian "The Quiet Assassin" French scored five tries out of eleven, and then the weather put a halt on proceedings for nigh on a month. After that we lost the next game to Featherstone but then we went to Barrow in the second round and beat them 30-6.'

The weather had worked in Castleford's favour and the next round was the following Sunday, against the mighty Wigan away. Kevin was colossal in this game as was everyone and the 10-2 victory over the Lancashire giants caused reverberations throughout the game. Next up, the following Sunday, a return to Wigan for the semifinal against Oldham. This looked like it could be a tricky one and so it proved. They had some stars in their squad, Dave Hobbs, Mick Worrell, Ray Ashton, Des Foy and the Liddiard brothers were all match winners in their own right. It was tough and scary right up to seventy minutes then Bob Beardmore scored and Cas held on. I recall Gary Lord saying later that three Stanley lads were on their way to Wembley meaning Kevin, myself and he. I quickly reminded him that the final was six weeks away; a lot could happen before then.

When Mal Reilly announced the team for the final in the Castleford dressing room, it was inevitable that someone would be disappointed at not being chosen. However most accepted Mal's choice with dignity and only one player demonstrated any petulance, which probably endorsed the decision to omit him. And while the fit of pique did not go unnoticed by the team, it seemed to have a galvanising effect. I think it made all the others aware of how fortunate they were and added an extra cog to the wheel of resolve each player would need when the time came.

There were to be other disappointments within the thirteen players and four subs yet Malcolm wasn't afraid of making the tough calls when needed. After all, when you reach a Wembley final, there are no second chances and it was his first visit to the twin towers as a coach, he was fully aware the responsibilities lay with more than just the players. The fans, committees and sponsors, all wanted a say in the team selection but Mal was having none of it. He had his own game plan which was wholeheartedly endorsed by John Kear and myself and which we hoped may have given him some comfort. As for Kevin, it was his first Wembley Cup final, he had suffered the heartbreak of semifinal defeat against Hull at Elland Road in 1983 and against the Airlie Birds again two seasons later after a 10-10 draw resulted in a 22-16 defeat at Headingley. As explained before, fellow finalists Hull KR, were something of a bogey side for Cas. Equal in almost every department but with a great coach in Roger Millward, an astute man and very likely aware of any weaknesses Cas may have on the day.

Hull KR went into the match as favourites, which is exactly how Cas wanted it. Fans and media alike were making predictions and comparisons of their champions elect; Gavin Millar against Ian French, Watkinson versus Kevin Beardmore, the two stand off halves Dorahy and Joyner, the two leaders in the boiler house Johnston against Kevin Ward. Would the prompting and probing of Paul Harkin curtail the silky skills of Bob Beardmore? It all augured well for a classic final and that's what we got, a nail biter right up to the finish when a conversion attempt in the dying minutes failed by inches to leave Cas with the spoils. Kevin made a vital contribution slipping a telling pass out of the tackle to put Tony Marchant on a sizzling sixty-five metre gallop to the line, where he threw a sublime dummy to score untouched for that first try. A lot of hard work was involved by both teams and tireless, sometimes frantic play, entertained the live 82,134 audience, who paid, a then, world record in turnstile receipts of £780,000. The turnabout score of 7-6 to Cas was indicative of the tight tussle, yet history was to prove, as with Tony's try, that it's the influential people who unlock the doors to the vaults and in Tony's case, it was Kevin's telling pass which set him on his way. The next time it was John Joyner, his pre-planned inside ball released the elusive explosive Aboriginal winger James 'Jamie' Sandy. His exhilarating turn of foot completely surprised George Fairbairn who valiantly tried to recover but Jamie got the ball down in the corner for a crucial score, despite being engulfed by defenders. Hull KR kept in touch with the game through two tries by Gary Prohm but the man who was rightly the Lance Todd winner, Bob Beardmore, opened the Hull KR defence with a delicate chip n' chase to score, which Martin Ketteridge just failed to convert. John Joyner would argue later that Cas were worthy winners and that it should not have gone to the wire, but it did and only Bob Beardmore's drop goal separated two very committed teams.

The proverbial celebrations followed well into the early hours, Kevin ruefully reflects; 'We were a good team and I honestly was never in fear of losing.'

'Well I was,' I replied, 'and I said a little prayer on the touchline side.'

That night the hotel was awash with joyous faces and many of the Castleford entourage achieved a state of total inebriation. I recall John Kear fell in a heap in a palm tree type shrub and needed help to extricate himself, that said, most of us were also in a similar intoxicated state.

'A day to remember Kevin?'

'Certainly was Dave, certainly was, and then the celebrations went on and on. It was a brilliant feeling when we paraded the trophy through Cas in that open top bus. The fans were ecstatic; you can understand why each club is desperate to win the Challenge Cup.'

'Certainly can Kevin, certainly can.'

12

The Battle of Belle Vue

'Kevin, what would you say was the most important moment in your playing career?'

'Hmm, let me think. I guess when I was given a chance against the Aussies in 1986. Even though we got beat in each test I held my place and that established me. It seemed to be a long time coming, especially after that one game against France in 1984, but I was given another chance and I took it. I had been playing well for a long time but for some reason my face just didn't fit, in fact it was because I was playing well with Cas that I didn't despair for too long. Cas were paying me and I had a job to do, just the same as I had a job to do 8 am till 5 pm. I had bills to pay, it is a great motivator, the difference of living in the comfort zone or not.'

'Is that what motivated you Kevin?'

'I looked at it this way, if success came about through pride and ambition then the money would follow.'

'And did it?'

'Yes, but not like today's players get paid. I'm not jealous, I have a nice house, a car and a few quid in the bank and my son Richard goes to a good school, so I'm happy that rugby has made our life more comfortable. We're not rich or anything and we still have to work, and to be honest, I worry some times how long I can keep doing a physical job in the building trade. One thing is for certain, I've made sure Richard knows about the hard work and sacrifices we've made to get where we are.'

'No pain, no gain Kevin.'

'That's true.'

'Do you ever reflect and realise how proud people are of your achievements Kevin?'

'No not really, I don't give it much thought these days.'

'Well I'm sure the people of Stanley are very proud of you, after all you were an achiever, a sporting hero, you did something that others aspire to.'

'Oh I used to think about things like that when I played and we had won something, like when I was all those miles away from home after the Grand Final win, I thought of my mum and dad and my family, also my roots, I've never forgotten them. I used to put it in this order, I told the Aussie media I came from Bottomboat, Stanley, near Wakefield, Yorkshire, England, but all that came out in print was this pommy or that pommy says this or that. It used to piss me off a bit but maybe this book will put things in perspective. I don't brag, but I'm no less proud of my origins than you or say George Duffield, Barry Hoban or your Denise, all who like you say have been sporting achievers that worked hard to get where they wanted to be.'

I am quick to point out that it's not a competition between villagers, I accept that all deserve praise and I also remind him that he is not the first Stanley lad to be deemed worthy of a place as prop for St Helens. Kevin's back straightens, a quizzical look appears on his face, 'Go on then, who?' He demands.

'John Lindley, a Lime Pit Laner played centre then in the pack for Wakefield in the late 50s, he was a very good tough player and Saints wanted a number 10 so they signed him. He was highly rated, tough as teak. Legend has it he and Jim

Drake, the Hull number 10, both got sent off at Belle Vue for fighting and it continued all the way up the tunnel and back to the dressing room. John suffered a knee injury after about ten games and it finished him and he like you Kev, a Stanley Ranger.'

'You know some stuff Sammy.'

'And you're not the first Bottomboater to play for St Helens either, or to tour, or to play for Great Britain.'

'I have a feeling I'm going to get to know who.'

'You betcha Kevin, his name was Brian Briggs.'

'Oh of course. I knew Brian, it had slipped my mind, he died a few years ago in Australia.'

'I think you're right God bless him. He was a real character; he moved from Saints to Wakefield and played in the Battle of Belle Vue in the early sixties against the Aussie touring party. Him and that Aussie hooker had a right set to. I was in the crowd in that corner when the first ruckus broke out. It was at a scrum in the bottom corner of the Agbrigg Road end. Neil Fox and Reg Gasnier were sat on their haunches on the half way line, the rest were swapping punches. I can't remember who the Aussie hooker was though.'

'Why don't you ask your Malcolm, he was in the Trinity team that day so he should remember.'

'Okay, he's probably having a pint down at the Lee Moor, let's go see.'

Kevin and I stroll down to the Lee Moor public house and as predicted, Malcolm is in his usual seat. Even at sixty-three years old he still looks exceptionally fit and he is.

'Two pints of lager Arthur please.'

'I'll get them Arthur,' Malcolm says, genuinely pleased to

see us especially Kevin after such a long time. 'You'll not get much writing done in the pub you know.'

'We're not here to write but to research.' I reply.

'True,' Kevin says, raising his glass, 'plus a little inspiration.' He smiles broadly while wiping the froth from his mouth, his glass half-empty after his first sup.

I turn to Malcolm. 'Kevin and I were discussing Brian Briggs and the battle of Belle Vue, we thought it might interest his readers if you can recollect it for us.'

'I certainly can like it were yesterday. Brian Briggs had been having a running battle with their hooker, a short stocky bugger, hard as nails. Noel Kelly was his name, the selectors had paid respect to Wakefield by naming a test side against us, mind you, we nearly had a test side in those days. Wilky, Briggsy, Rocky Turner and Don Vines were all international forwards. It wasn't funny at the time but I can laugh about it now. It erupted at a scrum, I was at number 10 and only nineteen years old, then moments before the scrum formed Rocky whispered, "Open up a bit as you form," it all happened so fast, I did as I was told and left a space. To this day I don't know whether Brian or Rocky Turner threw that first punch but it landed with a right thud on that cocky little hooker - I say little - he was built like a tank. I thought World War Three had broken out, Billy Wilson their number 10 thought it was me and started his retribution by throwing two punches at me, then Rocky grabbed him in a head lock and shouted, "Hit the bastard Malc," so I let loose with a short flurry. It was mayhem, then next moment I ducked to avoid a haymaker from Thornett the big full back. It whistled over my head with a swishing sound. Next thing someone pulled me out, he had green and gold on, so I let go at him, it was Kenny Irvine the legendary winger, he intimated that he didn't want any truck with the proceedings. Then Rocky pulled me away and said, "Come on Malc we don't want to be getting involved in a brawl." I looked to my left and Brian Briggs and Noel Kelly were at it hammer and tong, they were the last to be separated. Brian had an eye swollen shut but he held out another five minutes before he left the field for treatment. Then there was another almighty bust up but this time it was personal between Briggsy and Kelly and everyone left them to it. The ref sent them both off which calmed things down a bit.

Thinking back, if Thornett had connected with that punch, I think I would have missed the civic reception at the town hall that night. Thankfully I came out of the game relatively unscathed but the Aussie lads looked well battered. Funny thing was, at the civic reception I was seated next to the Aussie tour manager and he was a real gent. During his speech he praised Wakefield Trinity and thanked them to a man for giving them the best preparation a touring team could ask for the forthcoming test. But he couldn't hide his disappointment at losing the fight as well as the game and he generously said so.'

Kevin and I had sat attentively listening to this first hand recollection of those historic moments in that glorious era.

'I wish I could get Kevin to open up like that, he would rather listen to reminiscences than offer up his own stories, it's like trying to get blood out of a stone.' I state to Malcolm.

'Well when he gets to my age, reminiscences are all you have and it's very pleasurable to hand them on occasionally.'

13

Johnny Got It Wrong

When Kevin recalls the big games, he never fails to mention the 1992 World Cup final against the indomitable Aussies. The game was taken to our capital and national stadium in a bold move by the powers that be. And bearing in mind it was billed as the Stones Bitter final it was also co-sponsored by British Coal, the final game in their era of sponsorship. A vociferous crowd booed relentlessly during the heady preliminaries, TUC secretary Norman Willis was in attendance but most of the consternation shown by the fans was aimed at Douglas Hurd as he was presented to the players before proceedings commenced. Many northern based supporters in the magnificent 73,000 crowd aired banners of protest at certain newspapers who they blamed for the election result that had culminated in many more of the dwindling band of miners losing their jobs. Other fans simply blacked out the British Coal logo on their shirts. Southern based journalists turned up in their droves, hopeful of making political exploitation of a secondary situation but while there were many people in the crowd from all walks of life loyal to the miners plight, the majority were just there to witness a game of rugby league, hopeful that the Mal Reilly and Phil Larder coached team could win this one-off epic encounter.

The game itself was the final piece of a four-year jigsaw, Great Britain qualifying on a superior points difference over

New Zealand. In the recent tour of the summer of 1992, Great Britain had taken on the Aussies in Brisbane and gone close to emulating their 1988 third test feat of actually beating Australia, finally losing narrowly 16-10. So as the final approached, many pundits thought it fair to assume that at Wembley, on home soil, this Mal Reilly inspired squad could turn the tables. It seemed a valid assumption considering those summer tourists had gone so close to recapturing the ashes. Phil Larder tipped Great Britain to win by seven points, Peter Tunks the opposite but the most controversial aspect had to be the selection of Kevin at number 8, a bold brave move by Mal Reilly, but as Kevin says things were going well for him with Saints.

'I was the form prop and although I'd withdrawn from the international scene I was not fazed at the thought of a comeback.'

Kevin's inclusion caused quite a stir with the Aussie media and the article by Malcolm Andrews at the time in the *League Express* and his interview with the legendary Johnny Raper was indicative of how he tried to reconcile a reason for Kevin's inclusion, indicating that Mal was only using Kevin to soften the Aussies up early on. Johnny was a test selector for the Aussies and he reasoned, 'Why else would you pick a thirty-five year old, there is no way he is going to last the eighty minutes. It's quite obvious Reilly wants Ward out there to knock our blokes about early on, I reckon things could get a bit nasty but if it does it will backfire on Britain. Those sort of tactics won't work, that sort of nonsense went out of the game years ago, you could get away with it in test matches in my time but you can't today'.

On reading this, if he did, I'm sure Mal Reilly would have had a chuckle, he knew Kevin inside out. The big man's presence and power might have been intimidatory but he was no thug. He could match the Aussies like for like and for a full eighty minutes if necessary - something he went out and proved.

Kevin hated subbing or being subbed, he saw it as an insult to his prowess and never could accept a tactical ploy as an excuse or an injection of purpose from the bench. It may have stemmed from an in-built inferiority complex emanating from many such people of working class backgrounds, the fear factor of failing a master or father and one thing is for sure, when Kevin donned that number 8 jersey, he wanted it to be for the whole eighty minutes, so in Kevin's opinion, Johnny Raper was way off the mark in his assessment.

The game itself did not do justice to a world record crowd for a test match. Thrilling artistic three-quarter play was non-existent for most of the game and although the forwards battled against each other remorselessly, it never became the ugly brawl predicted by Johnny Raper. Instead, it was a close fought yet cautious match where no more than two points separated the teams until the sixty-eighth minute. But then, as Kevin said in his post match statement, 'We relaxed for two seconds but it was long enough for them to score that crucial try.'

'That's how I recall it,' I say to Kevin, 'they brought on a creative sub in Kevin Walters, his craft unlocked Steve Renouf and John Devereux's weak misguided attempt to tackle Renouf allowed the match winning score at 10-6.'

'I think that's a bit rough on John Devereux.'

'Maybe Kevin but it's a harsh world in test match rugby, the World Cup was at stake, Carne and Hancock the Aussie wingers made seven and six tackles respectively with no misses, Offiah and Hunte made five and seven tackles with no misses and John Devereux made six with one miss. That momentary lapse in concentration and application was the difference, he should have gone low, instead he went high and a big price was paid.'

'Well I disagree Dave, what about Shaun Edwards getting sin binned, what about Alan Hunte losing the ball that led to the try. I just don't accept one man can be blamed in a team effort.'

'Okay Kevin, I concede, you've made your point.'

Kevin was obviously bitterly disappointed with this loss; in fact, it still shows on his face when he discusses the subject today. He knew what it was like to lose at Wembley having done so with St Helens against Wigan and that had been a real low point as he so dearly wanted it for his team-mates and the fans, but the World Cup Final was much worse. This loss was harder to take, not just for the lads and the fans or because it was on a world stage but for Malcolm Reilly, Phil Larder and the rest of the coaching staff. They deserved the trophy, they had put so much into the quest for victory only to get so close, yet at the end, receive so little in return.

Now that summer of the 1992 tour, Kevin wasn't even in the Great Britain squad having decided to retire from international rugby. According to the press this was to the advantage of the Aussies, indeed an article in the programme for the second test in Melbourne described the high regard in which Kevin was held. But then Ian Lucas of Wigan was almost decapitated and his resultant head injury caused him to be flown home. Now Kevin's form that season with Saints had warranted inclusion but he had not retracted his statement of international retirement, and yet word on the grapevine was that he was dying for one last crack at those Aussies. Kevin was one of a select chosen band who had actually experienced success against the Aussies, his Man of the Match performance in the first test of 1988 when Great Britain lost 17-6 alarmed the opposition and then he performed heroically in the final 26-12 test victory with the rag tag remnants of a squad. No doubt his presence would have been a bonus on tour, so I put the question to Kevin would he have liked another go at the Aussies?

'Well to be honest yes, I had enjoyed the season with Saints and I suppose the disappointment of losing to Wigan at Wembley made me realise I still wanted to play and win big matches. Then when Ian Lucas got poleaxed by Paul Harrogan I needed no more motivating, I made it known but I didn't get the phone call and that's what surprised me about being called up for the World Cup final at Wembley.'

'Have you any idea why you weren't contacted?'

'No, that's a question to ask someone else.'

'Do you think you could have made a difference?'

'I don't know, maybe.'

'Did it hurt you?'

'No, there were some good young players out there, Crooks, Skerrett, Harrison.'

'The Aussie media were saying you were the answer.'

'The Aussie media are always hyping things up, had Malcolm sent for me they would have slated him in the press, probably saying that he'd panicked and sent for a has-been. Anyway, Mal is an intelligent bloke so I'm sure he would have weighed up all the options.'

'But the fact that Harrogan flattened Lucas and got off with it spiced you up a bit?'

'No, the fact he had a green and gold jersey was all the

incentive I needed.'

'You saw no need to exact retribution then?'

'I just wanted us to beat them, that's what hurts an Aussie most, losing a game. I wasn't interested in going outside the rules, my record speaks for itself, almost 450 games and I was sent off only three times. I was dismissed for tripping, against Cas of all clubs, when Mike Ford wrong footed me; it wasn't malicious and he wasn't hurt, I just reacted to try and stop him. Then I was sent off for an instinctive outstretched arm which Bright Sodjie hung his chin on but was unscathed. And the only other was a punch in retaliation against Keith Rayne of Leeds which saw us both marched and Keith requiring several stitches. It was a changing era I played in Dave, when I started it was more physical but I didn't see any need to throw punches, I could make my mark just as well without resorting to that kind of behaviour.'

'Did you ever fear an opponent Kevin?'

'No never, the only things I fear in life are the things that might be out of my control, like something happening to my family. I was scared when they said I might lose my leg but never on a rugby field, I just played the game hard but to the rules.'

'So how did you feel when Johnny Raper insinuated you had been picked for the final just to rough up the opposition?'

'I knew he was talking bullshit, I've never been a biff and bash merchant and I certainly wasn't planning to be on for only the first twenty minutes.'

14

Unfair Tribunal

During my latest interview with Kevin I touch on the subject of spice, not sweets I hasten to add for those of northern origin, but spice for the book. Kevin is not forthcoming nor does he want to dwell on the subject matter, so I decided to tempt providence by pushing harder.

'You know Kevin, you are often quoted in the same breath, and quite rightly so, as Cliff Watson. He had some spice to offer in his career.'

'Such as?' snaps Kevin.

'Well the tale goes that he was last Englishman out of the dressing room as the Aussies filed out after half-time. Cliff had ruffled a few feathers in the first half with his abrasive style, so Aussie hard nut Peter Diamond smacked a smiling Cliff on the chin as he came out through the dressing room door. Then when Cliff belatedly joined the teams on the pitch, one of the Aussies told Cliff who had laid him one on. Cliff soon made his way to the wing and proceeded to lay into Diamond without any apparent justification. Conclusion, the ref sent Cliff off and the Aussies had a laugh at his expense. That's a bit of spice Kevin.'

'Well nobody ever lamped me in the dressing room.'

'What about when you were in your rebellious years as a young man, there must have been girlfriends Kevin, any spice then?'

'If you mention any of your bar staff by name Sammy, I'll

sue you, book or no book.'

'Wouldn't dream of it mate.'

'I'll tell you what was a bit of spice this week,' Kevin says, perking up. 'I visited the disability tribunal last Thursday and they assessed no deterioration in my leg that I broke and ended my playing days, so my money stays the same, £20 a week.'

'But I thought you said the pain is steadily worsening?'

'They can't measure pain with a tape and that's all the wise men used. I've been told that if I wasn't working it would strengthen my case.'

'How can you be expected to live on sick pay and that paltry pension while you fight for months to win an increase?'

'Exactly, so much for justice Dave, anyhow I can appeal.'

'But I bet you won't.'

'No, probably not.'

'Well I'm not voting Labour next time, they are no longer the party of the working man in Britain.'

'What makes you say that Dave?'

'Well they exploit the working man just like the capitalists did to our forefathers; there is nothing to choose between them.'

'So are you saying we should vote Liberal? Because the Tories are not an option, even I know that much.'

'No Kevin, that's not an option either, I guess you can liken it to a pint of Ale and the Liberals equate to what you spill.'

'And the Conservatives?'

'Oh they're akin to the vessel you drink from, more plastic than glass these days but still you need one.'

'And the Labour Party?'

'Labour is the ale, frothy, clear and tasty, yet it's addictive and expensive. But Labour now have us by the bollocks and they keep squeezing, just enough to keep the masses loyal and yet maintain and sustain power.'

'We are drifting into politics Dave, I'm basically happy with my lot; I have a nice house, a loving wife, a son in private education, and a nice car.'

'Yes mate I know, we are all Mr and Mrs Suburbia, but let's take the credit that's due, we've earned it. I think you're too modest at times Kevin, had you been born in a different period, say the time of the ancient Greeks, an athlete like you would have thrown the discuss from Athens to Mesopotamia - and don't ask where Mesopotamia is. Had you been born in the time of King Arthur you would have been a knight, maybe Sir Lancelot. And had you been born during the industrial revolution, say the son of a miner, you would have been a champion in the fight against oppression, a campaigner fighting for justice for the lowest regarded people in that society of the time. As it was you were born in Stanley during better times and you made something of yourself on the rugby pitch.'

'What the bloody hell are you going on about?'

'I guess I'm just pontificating but the point is me old mate, if you go to the swimming baths are you conscious that your leg is so disfigured?'

'Yes, naturally.'

'Is it the same say on the beach on holiday or in summer when in shorts?'

'Yes.'

'So would you agree it causes you mental anguish?'

'Well yes, I guess it does.'

'Now tell me, at work when on the building site, do you

tread warily on uneven ground or in footings or near machinery?'

'I do, constantly.'

'And if you catch the slightest knock on the damaged area, say some bricks or a scaffold pole or a batten what then?'

'It hurts like hell because there's no muscle to cushion it.'

'And at the tribunal, in their infinite wisdom they say you only warrant £20 a week despite you being injured in your work playing rugby. Tell me Kevin was there a solicitor on the panel?'

'Yes.'

'And a doctor?'

'There was.'

'Did you have a solicitor or anyone from the medical profession representing you?'

'No.'

'Hardly seems a fair tribunal mate.'

'No, I guess not.'

'Well it sounds to me that you need someone to fight your case, if you only win a slight increase it will be a moral victory and it will help others in the queue behind you. So my point is don't give up, appeal, it is your right, it is a right that was earned at a cost, so put yourself about a bit.'

'Hmm, I'll give it some thought.'

15

A Cool Lager, a Final Lost

Reminiscing is thirsty work especially when the outside temperature is approaching twenty-five degrees, so Mavis my wife raids the fridge for a couple of bottles of beer. Kevin and I take a break, we both wander outside where Kevin notices an article in that day's *Yorkshire Post* laid on top of the patio table. I had read the same piece earlier in the day so I seized the chance to raise the subject with Kevin who now was thoroughly absorbed with the text.

'What do you think Kevin?' I ask.

'I reckon the RFL are taking a calculated risk.'

The article refers to the refusal of Sky TV's offer of over fifty million for five years. Kevin takes another sip of cool lager he then states, 'It will bugger some people's weekends up with no televised rugby every Friday and Saturday.'

'It certainly will, including me, you and our Malc and many more in pubs and clubs around the country.'

'But I don't think Sky would want to lose rugby league because it would have world wide repercussions.'

'Yes but the game doesn't need this Russian roulette. Sky and the RFL have come a long way together in a short time, each needs the other.' I state.

'Maybe Sky should do a referendum of viewers asking if they will cough up a little more money in subscriptions to allow them to pass it on in an increased offer to the RFL.'

'Whoa, hang on Kev, that may seem simple but a lot of

people think Sky is expensive anyway, especially with the fierce competition between TV channels.'

'Well it was just a suggestion but I'll tell you what Dave, if the RFL think that by taking Super League off the telly it's going to increase attendances I reckon they'll get it wrong.'

'I agree Kevin so just hope it doesn't come to that. Now let's get back to some work, so tell me, you played at Wembley just twice at club level, how big a disappointment was the one with St Helens?'

'Massive, a huge hurtful experience is the only way I can explain it. Mike McClennan had us in the right frame of mind and we were totally convinced that we could turn Wigan over. We had had a hard run up to Wembley and we had lost the week before to Hull in the Premiership play-offs but I think the final was on a lot of people's minds over at the Boulevard. But then Wigan had also lost at home to Featherstone. Wigan had played ten games since the semifinal, we had only played five and rumours were rife that they were crippled by injury, many of them serious. They were favourites on paper but that suited us and our game plan was to take advantage of their injuries by staying with them until they died on their feet. Then we saw Hanley needed a fitness test before the game and we were lifted a little more. Kelvin Skerett was suspended, Joe Lydon was out injured, the news just continued to filter through, each time lifting us psychologically. In the game we came so close but we didn't deserve to win, early on we couldn't hold the bloody ball, then we lost Paul Loughlin and Phil Vievers, injured - both concussed. We knew Wigan would throw the kitchen sink at us, all we had to do was contain them and be patient. However, we paid the penalty for poor ball retention and we went in at half-time 12-0 down. We knew they were battle weary but what we hadn't counted on was so were we, then Andy Gregory dropped a goal early in the second half to make it 13-0 and still I thought we could win, especially after Alan Hunte scored and Bishop converted and then he kicked a penalty to make it 13-8. We were a try and goal from victory and ten minutes remained, so we threw everything and the kitchen sink back at them. But all credit to Wigan, they held us out.

'I remember at the end that there were very few players who had not taken a battering, both teams were bloodstained; Bernard Dwyer very nearly lost his ear it was so badly cut. Then when Ellery hoisted that trophy, that's when it struck home to me. I felt gutted, absolutely devastated. I just want to get out of it, away from it all. Winning lifts you, defeat deflates, yes I think that was my most hurtful club defeat ever.'

'Would you rather have gone out in the semi?'

'Oh no, no way, I enjoyed beating Widnes in the semi. George Mann and myself had big games, in fact our pack dominated Widnes. No, to lose a semi is equally painful and I had my bellyful of those with Cas. At least when you make a final you can savour the occasion. I guess I was a bit emotional because I wanted it for the fans. I suppose each time I turned out for Saints I wanted to reward them for welcoming me to the club. You know Dave, when the news broke that I had signed for Saints, a lot of people criticised the club saying I was too old and past it, so I wanted to silence them.'

'I didn't realise Kevin, I thought the transition from Cas to Saints was smooth.'

'No, I had to convert a few sceptics, every club has them and I enjoyed winning them over, they are fanatical yet they're brilliant people.'

'As they are in Cas Kevin.'

'Very true Dave, I still have regrets that I never got a chance to say goodbye to the Wheldon Road fans properly, I mean from the pitch. My last game was as a sub at Headingley and I didn't sign for Saints until July in the close season.'

'Any regrets other than that Kevin?'

'Not really, a new coach comes in and he's bound to change things. I was disappointed that David Poulter backed Darryl so much but these things happen and with hindsight I'm glad I made the move, controversial or not.'

'Time to break it up mate.'

'Yes, I'll see you next week.'

16

Good Friday, Bad Friday

When Kevin travelled over to Wigan on Good Friday morning 1993, it was just another game. A big game mind you, although at thirty-four years of age and with a long illustrious career behind him, he wasn't nervous or apprehensive. He had no special thoughts as he crossed the Pennine hills other than it was going to be a tough encounter, as the Wigan V Saints derbies invariably were. Kevin quietly mused to himself that a good performance that day would endear him a little more to the St Helens hierarchy, the season was coming to a close, so too was his three year contract and he was determined to win another two year one and maybe, just maybe, another crack at the old enemy the Aussies. He had no fears, no premonitions of disaster; he carried his holdall and a steely determination to impose his presence on his much daunted, highly respected opponents.

On stripping and readying himself there was a noticeable air of confidence in the dressing room, each player quietly going about their preparations. Rub downs, strappings, the odd injection of an unpronounceable prescribed and allowed painkiller, already common practice in the game at that time. Some players were quiet, others chatted, each aware of his team-mates' quirks. But little did Kevin or anyone else realise that this was to be the last time he would don his kit, strap his ankles and his wrist and lace up his boots. After all, this was just a normal match day so he was indifferent to the possibility that anything could go seriously awry. Oh a burst nose, a few bruises and the odd muscle tear were commonplace and accepted as part and parcel, but nothing even remotely career threatening ever crossed the player's thoughts at this stage. Stepping out into the cauldron of Central Park for a Good Friday traditional derby was a special experience. The players would be privately reminding themselves of last minute instructions, 'Out play my immediate opponent, control my aggression, show respect for ball possession'. Kevin would be reminding himself of all these things plus others, such as; 'Make the hard yards, lead by example,' but little did he know then that these last few recollections were to cost him dear.

It happened when the game was finely poised at eight points all, midway through the second half. It had been every bit as tough as expected and no doubt many of the players were tiring but some have the ability to dip into extra reserves of energy and Kevin was one such player and this was one such moment. St Helens were working the ball out of their defensive quarter. Kevin wound himself up, launched himself into a powerful surge and he hurtled his mighty frame at the redoubtable Wigan defence. As his left foot hit the ground carrying his whole seventeen and a half stone body, a Wigan defender simultaneously launched himself with a brave, almost suicidal yet copybook tackle, his shoulder crashing into Kevin's momentarily static left leg, a sickening crack echoed around a stunned stadium. Millions of TV pundits leaped from their armchairs, the sight of this magnificent athlete crumbling, as if in slow motion into a pain etched heap was nauseating. Quiet descended over Central Park and even the most vocal of the opposition fans were silent. Then as Kevin was ministered and stretchered from the arena, the whole stadium resounded with respectful and concerned applause. The extent of Kevin's injury was more apparent to the TV audience, replay after replay vividly showed his leg snapping as if a mere twig. The sight of Kevin's face as the pain and shock instantly sped to his brain was one that most viewers will long remember.

The game continued while Kevin lay in a corridor awaiting an ambulance, the injury shocked all the players yet Saints used it as a spur rather than capitulating, each member of the team showed tremendous character and they earned a respectable draw, commendable in such circumstances. Afterwards all quickly returned to the dressing room to console their fallen team-mate. Alas Kevin was already on his way to Wigan Infirmary.

When Kevin had arrived in the dressing room, stretcher born from the field, he was instantly given a pain killing injection but in Kevin's own words, 'It didn't bloody work, the pain was excruciating. I sat up on the stretcher and gazed at my leg, my foot was facing the wrong way round. I instinctively leant forward, took hold of my foot and tried to twist it back, it seemed the normal thing to do but I fell back screaming in agony. The foot when I released it, flopped into its original position, then sweat began to ooze from my face and I felt sick deep inside my stomach. The pain just got worse, I noticed people milling about, nosing, trying to catch a peek and then turning and shaking their heads, this was no real comfort. My emotions were mixed; I felt a surge of anger as the Doc cut my boot away. Little did I realise then, as he threw the tattered remnants to the floor, that he was hanging them up forever. The sock came next, soaked in blood; it was carefully cut and peeled away to expose the wound and protruding bone. Once again I turned away as the nausea came back. Then the doc could do nothing further so he placed a white sheet over the injury and I had no alternative but to wait to be transferred to hospital.

'When I arrived at Wigan Infirmary, I was told I would be going for a clean up and manipulation. I thought that sounds so simple the way the nurse glibly pronounced it and although I was still in pain, she did put me more at ease. Then twice I was wheeled into theatre and twice straight back out. First time a car crash casualty took priority, then a stabbing victim and finally in the early hours of Saturday morning, I was put to sleep. When I woke up, I was in a small ward with a pot on my leg up to above the knee. Then as I slowly came to my senses, the pain began to return, but this time it seemed to be the whole of my lower leg. It was throbbing so much it felt as if it was going to burst the pot, the pressure was agonising. During that morning, Saints chairman Eric Latham visited me, he was concerned for me and arranged for a transfer into a private hospital back in St Helens.'

Kevin's leg by this time had swollen so much that the doctor at the private hospital ordered the pot removed and the sight of a leg so badly swollen and black necessitated another transfer, this time to Whiston. In technical terms Kevin had developed compartment syndrome where infection had caused the tissues in his leg to swell which then restricted the blood flow inside his plaster cast and caused damage to the nerves and muscles. At Whiston, Kevin was rushed into theatre so the surgeon could make an eighteen-inch long incision in his leg down to the bone. The wound would be kept open to allow the swollen tissues to drain. Kevin was returned to the hospital ward and a tent erected over his opened leg. Lack of sleep due to the pain was testing his resolve, yet he remained optimistic that these setbacks were minor hiccups. But at this time it had not crossed his thoughts of what lay ahead, he was determined that after a couple of months in a plaster cast he would start his rehabilitation.

Kevin had always relished training and he consoled himself that he could have a whole summer of intense physiotherapy and weights to get back to match fitness for the new season. He harboured no thoughts of quitting, or that the injury might curtail his career. Some may argue that he was being naive, possibly so, but Kevin would argue a defeatist attitude would do him no good at all. He was still enthusiastic for the game, which I'm sure is a vital factor in prolonging a player's career. To Kevin it was simple, he asserted at the time: 'I have a badly broken leg, so what, it has happened to others and it will happen again.' Obviously he had no intentions of letting self doubt jeopardise his recovery.

Occasionally in moments when he was alone, Kevin would take a peek under his tent, the leg was swollen and black in colour from knee to toe. He could see the inner workings of his leg, the bone, muscles and tendons in the deep slit opened by the surgeon's blade. Visitors came and offered consolation and some were brave enough to take a curious look, but most wished they hadn't and reeled back horrified at the sight. Then after a few days the swelling increased requiring another theatre visit for further surgery, but this time, unable to stem the flow of blood, the surgeon broke the grave news to Kevin that unless the flow ceased by its own accord, they would have to amputate. He was told the next hour was vital.

I asked Kevin how he felt at that point.

'It was a bloody shock; I didn't really know what to think. I remember feeling absolutely frantic; I couldn't believe it was happening to me, I wanted to turn back the clock and avoid that tackle at Central Park, I was worried what would happen to me if I lost my leg and I was worried how it would affect Margaret and Richard. I just wanted someone to wake me up out of a bad dream!'

Fortunately, as it turned out, the blood flow gradually subsided and Kevin's leg was saved. Several days passed before Kevin was informed that once again he was to return to theatre, only this time it would be an operation to insert a steel rod from just below his kneecap to the ankle. Afterwards all appeared to be going well, although still immobile and the deep incision remaining open, Kevin was a little more upbeat. His doctors then stated he needed another theatre visit, this time for skin grafts over the gaping wound. While he recovered from the grafts, Kevin began to look forward to his discharge from Whiston as travelling for Margaret and Richard was difficult and time consuming. He was also eager to begin physiotherapy and ultimately start training again as by now he had already lost a month in hospital.

The news of his discharge lifted his and everyone's spirits, St Helens showed their support for Kevin by offering him a new one-season contract for £6,000. At this stage everyone was optimistic about the future.

Kevin began his physiotherapy under the watchful eye and guidance of Lee Robinson, a much-respected Wakefield based physiotherapist. Lee liaised with the St Helens physio and the club surgeon and Kevin continued to travel to Whiston Hospital for checkups and treatment. But as the months passed, Kevin became increasingly more frustrated at the slow progress, he was walking unaided but had a pronounced limp, he also complained about feeling unwell. Lee Robinson was becoming equally concerned, especially with a small area of skin which had begun to blister and weep near to the break area so Kevin agreed to visit another specialist, a Mr Lawton in Leeds.

The outcome of this meeting was that Mr Lawton needed permission from the Saints club doctor and his records transferred over from Whiston, unfortunately, valuable time elapsed before his records finally arrived. Mr Lawton diagnosed an infection and a despondent Kevin returned once again to theatre for an exploratory operation. Mr Lawton cleaned up the infected area, removed some floating bone fragments and cut away some dead muscle, but one can imagine Kevin's surprise the next day when the surgeon visited his bedside with a small jar containing this foreign matter and also two drill bits, or at least the tips of them!

Kevin's natural reaction was anger, muted by the fact that maybe now, with the aid of some strong antibiotics, he was at last on the road to recovery; the new found optimism fuelled by confidence in Mr Lawton's assurances that they would get it right. Mr Lawton had removed the rod from Kevin's leg in the operation and attached an outside fixator, a type of external metal scaffold screwed into the leg for stabilisation and to enable the healing process to take place. But the next three to four months passed by agonisingly slowly and Kevin was becoming increasingly aware that the new season would not see him don his coveted number 8 jersey, yet he still remained optimistic; maybe next year. The next few months he knew would be vital for him; he must keep his positive approach. However, one can imagine his devastation at the news that the long course of antibiotics, rest and elevation had proved fruitless. The vital healing process and calcification he had hoped for had failed to materialise, the leg had hardly improved and he was back to square one.

Saints organised a testimonial match for Kevin, and other fund-raising events raised him a few thousand pounds, for which he remains eternally grateful. But it was becoming increasingly obvious that his career was over. Kevin tried to console himself that at least it had happened at the close of his career and not earlier, small consolation in the circumstances. Kevin once again returned to see Mr Lawton, he was advocating a bone graft, a long painful process but probably the only course available. However, he suggested that a consultation with a plastic surgeon, a Mr Batchelor, might offer an alternative. Mr Batchelor duly met Kevin and he prognosticated a free flap operation incorporating the removal of a piece of muscle from Kevin's shoulder which would be implanted between the bone and remaining muscle in his leg, and which if successful would strengthen the leg and allow calcification of the bones.

Kevin's thoughts were now on saving his leg, the slow process of coming to terms of life without rugby paled in comparison with the fears he harboured about his future as a prospective cripple. Gallantly he entered hospital again for the free flap surgery, his ninth visit to theatre since that fateful holy day that now seemed such a long time ago.

Kevin emerged from this operation, his last to date, with a steely determination to recover and so he did, although he still had to endure pain, discomfort and mental anguish. However, this time the healing process slowly advanced and Kevin painstakingly rebuilt the remnants of his decimated lower limb. His limp gradually eased and, as Margaret says, his smile re-emerged. The saga had tested his resilience to the full, the monetary losses can only be estimated, the mental anguish and physical strains may live with him forever and who can assess what price he may pay later in life for the two and a half years it took Kevin to recover to his present condition.

Kevin has a legacy to bear, he is now limited in his ability to walk any great distance, running and training are an impossibility and playing rugby league is simply out of the question. He returned reluctantly to his job on the building sites where he found the manual labour equally as energy sapping and painful as the hours of physiotherapy, as naturally, his mighty frame had become a little soft through his sustained incapacity. But I think what still upsets Kevin (and I know it certainly galls me) is that he only received a paltry £5,000 from the Rugby Football League and he's only paid £20 a week industrial injury pension – what a way to treat one of our fallen heroes!

To say Kevin is slightly pissed off about the whole affair is an understatement. It was suggested to him that he had a strong cases for redress for negligence in his treatment, but Kevin is first and foremost an honourable working class lad, reluctant to blame or risk offending the many loyal people who nursed him so diligently. Kevin adds, 'I'm miffed for myself and other professional players and amateurs who suffer through the governing body's reluctance to provide sufficient insurance cover.' Kevin believed he was insured but he wasn't. He continues, 'I just hope players today are covered better than I was, I wouldn't want anyone to have to go through what I suffered and still have to worry about money.' He adds, 'Cas signed me for £3,000 and twelve years later they sell me on for £82,000, smart business some might say. Saints naturally insure against losing my services and get a payout when they do. I am very grateful to St Helens, they showed faith when they signed me and hopefully they appreciated the effort I put in during my eighty-nine games. I am also very grateful for their efforts and consideration when I broke my leg, yet at the end of the day, I am the one who paid the ultimate price and I will be retired a long time.'

If we didn't have the players who love the game so dearly, we would not have a Super League, and as often said before; the fat cats are still getting fatter. And when I hear talk that the players are earning too much, I grind my teeth in frustration; without the players, the television companies do not have a product to sell to the world and the RFL does not have a product to sell to television. I believe the players give better value than they are paid for, I mean, just look at how much the top football players earn, yet when someone touches them on the pitch, they go down in a heap as if they had been shot. If rugby league players followed that fashion, there would be ambulances everywhere and I don't think there would be enough subs to finish a game. But no, rugby league players regularly turn out week in week out carrying injuries that would make lesser men wince. Just look at Leon Pryce in the recent Leeds Rhinos V Bradford Bulls derby. Leon received a sternum injury in the previous game and was told he would be out for three weeks, but six days later he started the match at Headingley because he was the least injured of the senior stand offs in the Bradford side. By half-time and after several crunching tackles, Leon Pryce could barely stand and was subbed but it underlines the grit and determination that the players give to the sport and they are worth every penny they're paid - and a lot more too. And when you look at the price that Kevin has had to pay, well the recompense for all the pain, the distress and the permanent incapacity doesn't even come close to being fair.

17

Two Paths, Choosing the Right One

Kevin and I are meeting less and less these days; it's as though the book we are writing is like a game of rugby entering the final quarter. But with the help of his old mate Peter Harrison, who has kindly helped out with some of the research and provided surplus interview material direct from Kevin, we're still making progress. I need Kevin only to answer questions on some of the minor details; but it is still good to see him and pass the time of day.

There was, however, a time in Kevin's life when he seemed to be speeding along the road to nowhere, I guess at that time he lacked any real goals and was in need of a push in the right direction. It was early in his professional career, he had made the Castleford first team and with it had newfound wealth, an income that shamed his meagre pit earnings. Kevin was treading the same pathway that many more before him had. Sport was or seemed to be a ticket away from the mine, which, despite the camaraderie, he freely admits he loathed. Who could really blame him, his winning pay packet in cash in those days was three times that of a collier. Absenteeism was rife throughout the coalfields, especially on Mondays when a culmination of three consecutive day and night sessions on the booze caused many to ignore any knockers-up in the early hours of the first working day of the week. Inevitably, when the pub doors opened at 11 o'clock in Wakefield town centre, small groups of men from different pits around the area would quickly vanish indoors into the pub of their choice. To some it was a weekly ritual, to others a less frequent occurrence. For some of the miners four shifts was enough and all their failing lungs and aching bodies could cope with, to others, especially the young bucks, it was nothing a double shift couldn't put right later in the week. And for the diligent ones who had risen at 4 am and fulfilled their given quota, these men would join their comrades a little later, washed and changed, yet retaining the telltale black mascara ingrained in the eyelashes. One could recognise the colliers from the builders and the equally definitive city slickers, the conmen, businessmen, newsmen, all to a man downing pint after pint of the foaming nectar.

Wakefield on a Monday lunchtime was a hubbub of activity, a stolen session for many, of which Kevin was occasionally one. The drinking-working man was a creature of habit and the usual establishment was the Black Rock Hotel. This was the early nineteen eighties, Kevin had worn his moderation hat for three sometimes four days prior to playing, but now it was time to enjoy himself. Be it myself, Peter, Bleggsy, Rusty or whoever, Kevin was not short of friends in those days, and when Kevin joined us, we would utter the words, 'Are you having one mate?' which was usually greeted by a response such as, 'Go on then, I'll let you twist my arm.'

As midday approached, the numbers would increase, jovial men all with a tale to tell, some old some new. Kevin often held centre stage, responding in his own inimitable style to the banter or mickey taking which was constant and shared. I recall one such Monday when Kevin's words brought silence to the group:

'Have you heard about Nipper then?'

'No,' came the unified response.

'What about Nipper?' I asked Kevin.

'He's in big trouble,' Kevin replied, 'he went to catch a bus to work early Friday morning, then he had a brainstorm, he let the bus go, then crossed the road and got on Selby bus going t'other way.'

'What shift was he on?' Bleggsy asked.

'Days, 7 o'clock, only problem he left his snap tin on t'bus and went on a bender in Selby.'

'So?'

'Well the conductor knew where he lived so on a return trip she dropped his snap tin off at their house. Nipper called in the Wagon for a last pint at 5 o'clock then went home as if it was a normal day.' Smiles are breaking out as Kevin is about to conclude this jewelled snippet and everyone is starting to see where the story is leading. Kevin continued, 'Their lass asks him where his snap tin is. He tells her he left it darn't pit. "You bloody liar," she said, "fucking Selby bus dun't go on your coalface." He ran out the house fast as his legs could carry him.' As the laughter died down Kevin concluded: 'He's serving a month with no sex.'

'Poor bugger it'll break his heart!' added Rusty.

Kevin then sat back, contented that his tale, his juicy tit-bit turned out so entertaining for every word was true. But many of these lads did not spend their precious hours simply on idle banter, many could and did hold intelligent discussions on a multitude of topics. All had gone to comprehensive schools and a good number could have continued in education through university, no doubt outsiders would assume that by going down the pit it indicated a lack of intellect, but in many cases nothing could be further from the truth. The fact of the matter was that if you were a son of a miner, there was a job for you. However, if the chain was broken by only one generation, then so was the guarantee of employment. Now some of these lads had a good few years' service in and now they were beginning to become concerned for their futures. The word was out that the government and coal bosses had other plans for the mining industry and this uncertainty fuelled a number of heated discussions, many of which were broken up by the sound of old Fred the Foot hollering at the top of his voice as he limped round the pub collecting empty glasses from the tables. 'Come on you idle bastards, fuck off somewhere else, the landlord rang time twenty minutes ago.'

'Any chance of afters Fred?'

'Don't ask me, ask Phil he's the gaffer. And anyway you bleedin colliers don't know when you've had enough; I'd sack yer'all if it were owt to do with me.'

Fred would continue with his tirade as he washed glass after glass. If we were fortunate and Phil allowed us the treat of a session after, Fred would once again strike up, 'You're just like your fathers; fucking alcoholics.'

Phil would intervene, 'Fred these are my customers you're talking to, you can't call them alcoholics.'

'Redfern you can bollocks as well, I'm off for me bus.'

'You'll be getting a solicitor's letter one of these days Fred,' one of the lads once joked. To which in turn Fred retorted, 'There's none of yer can sign your own fucking names, yer thick buggers, let alone commission a bloody solicitor.' At which everyone in the place fell about laughing. Fred then limped out to catch his bus but sure enough, he was back at his glass-washing post the next and every lunchtime until he passed away - a character truly beyond his time.

The Monday sessions had truly become a ritual, and usually when Kevin was there, Peter Harrison wasn't far away either. They had been school chums, teenage pals and were now grown men and still best mates. Kevin and Peter were inseparable and their antics were usually lively and fuelled by too much beer. After one such session which finished at the New York Bar, both were the worse for wear, fortunately they left the premises before the police arrived. Around this time, Kevin met Margaret, his wife-to-be and as with most young couples, the waters were at first a little stormy. The disputes were usually fuelled by his lively drinking sessions with Peter, but fortunately thanks to Margaret's sensible influence, Kevin started mending his ways. The wild days and nights with Peter diminished until finally the umbilical cord was cut. Margaret began to mould something out of her adored lump of granite and it was no coincidence that the hero of the Wheldon Road public began to make people within the game take note. Everyone wanted a piece of Kevin. Mal Reilly quite rightly earned a piece but in this book, the unsung heroine was Margaret. She got what she wanted, her man, and in doing so she helped support and guide him in his tremendous sporting career. A woman of substance who underpinned all that the great man achieved, together they conquered the world of rugby league from Castleford to Australia and back to St Helens. And more importantly, they built a life, a fine home and happiness.

18

A Night of Praise

When Kevin was given a testimonial dinner at St Helens, it was obviously tinged with sadness. It was now accepted by both the club and Kevin, that even by some kind of miracle should his leg recover, the fact that over two years had elapsed and he was now the wrong side of thirty-seven, father time had finally overtaken him and his sporting career was now over.

The price Saints had paid of £80,000 for a thirty-three year old prop in 1990 was testimony enough of the esteem and high regard he commanded and whilst many of the people who attended that testimonial dinner were from St Helens, there were also many rugby league personalities who simply wanted to be present to mark the occasion and say in years to come I was there.

Eric Ashton the St Helens chairman, himself a former great, is quoted as saying of Kevin, 'Make no mistake, Kevin Ward is one of the greats of rugby league and the doors of St Helens Rugby League Club will always be open to him.' That night the Beeches Club was full to capacity as others extolled the praises for Kevin. Knowing Kevin, I reckon he would have received the plaudits humbly, proud to be mentioned alongside the great Saints players of the past, legends like Cliff Watson, Tom Van Vollenhoven, Duggie 'Iron Man' Greenall and the irrepressible Alex Murphy. All of these were players who possessed that certain something that made them special, not just skill and ability but character and determination as well.

The consensus that night was that Kevin was undoubtedly the best prop to wear a Saints jersey since Cliff Watson and there have been some good ones, Chisnall, Warlow, Burke, Murphy to name but a few. Indeed the same could be said of Kevin at Castleford for only Dennis Hartley could be mentioned in the same breath up to the advent of Super League. And when Glen Dwyer travelled over from Australia to meet his heroes, the likes of Murphy, Karalius and Ashton, he would not be content until he had met Kevin.

But that night at the Beeches, the tributes came from the best in the game. Lee Crooks spoke a few profound words; 'Kevin is up there amongst the greatest ever front rowers. I've never known any with his power, sheer power, no one to touch him.' Bobby Goulding who had faced Kevin when hooking for Wigan said; 'He was awesome, a guy you didn't want to get the wrong side of, he had a quality that money couldn't buy, the respect of everyone in the game.' And George Mann who packed alongside Kevin was quoted; 'To play with Kevin was a privilege, I would do anything for him, he never took a backward step, he fought alongside me in the trenches trying to win every game regardless of the odds, it produced a tremendous camaraderie between us, a special bond.'

High praises indeed, all from genuine people about a genuine guy; Kevin has touched people around the globe, always prepared to make time when kids ask for autographs, willing to enter into conversation with fans and happy to stand for photos, the little things that people remember will endear him forever.

During his St Helens career Kevin soon converted the

doubters about the wisdom in signing a thirty-three year old, it can also be claimed with justification, that of the many star quality players who pulled on a Saints shirt for what can only be described as a short career, Kevin stands alongside only one or two greats such as Mal Meninga, the legendary Aussie powerhouse centre, for the impact made on both media and fans alike. Of the eighty-nine times he represented St Helens, a club of which he always speaks of in glowing terms, he featured in three draws, uncannily all were eight points to eight, Leeds away October 1991, Castleford away March 1992, and his last game ever, Wigan away April 1993 and in all three of these draws he wore the number 8 jersey. But 8 or 10 it mattered not to Kevin, he featured fifty-five times at number 10, and he subbed only three times, with the remaining thirty-one appearances at number 8. Of the total eighty-nine games he featured in, fifty-nine were victorious ones, which by my calculations is a sixty-six percent winning ratio and no mean feat, especially when considering that thirty-two were cup ties. And Kevin's statistics are reinforced when it's considered that over fifty percent of his games with St Helens were against the top sides of those three seasons: Hull, Hull KR, Leeds and Cas in Yorkshire and Warrington, Widnes and Wigan on the west side of the Pennines. In fact Kevin's fateful last appearance was his twelfth game against Wigan, the most respected yet bitterest of rivals, proof if needed that he was always up for the big games.

Nowadays ten years on from his enforced retirement, one has only to check back through the media records to understand the impact Kevin had on the scribes of those times. Comments such as: 'Ward's Herculean performance' or 'Mighty Ward's power turns game' and 'A colossus display'. I'm sure the Saints fans who were there still drool over the memory of many of Kevin's performances and probably none more so than the Lancashire Cup semifinal of 1991 at home against Wigan. The Saints fans in numbers witnessed the magnificence of Kevin at full throttle in a 28-16 victory. Then Kevin maintained his form, as did the team, to win the final 24-14 against Rochdale Hornets and a Lancashire medal to add to his much-prized collection.

Following Kevin's dramatic leg-break incident, Saints went on to win the Premiership Trophy 10-4 against Wigan, the thirteenth meeting between the two clubs in his time at St Helens. And while Kevin had played in all the previous twelve matches, he was on the winning side only twice but he makes no apology for marking Wigan out for a special rating:

'The Wigan-Saints derbies were the most intense club games I ever played in, more so than Castleford V Leeds, or Castleford V Featherstone or even Manly V Norths, nothing compares. The fans' passion is infectious, the rivalry borders on maniacal, and the atmosphere, with a sea of red and white fanatical fans on both sides has to be experienced to be believed.'

'Did you enjoy the experience?' I ask

'I don't know if enjoy would be the right word but I wouldn't have missed it for anything.'

19

A Night of Nostalgia

'I'd be delighted.' Those were my words when my son Dean asked me if I wanted to be a guest at Castleford Tigers. A three course meal for the sake of a few words into the microphone seemed like an offer too good to refuse, but little did I know that during the deliberations the indomitable Mick Morgan would be running a picture quiz, twenty-four faces, twenty-three of which I recognised which won me first prize of a dinner for two back at the restaurant at the match against London Broncos. My immediate thought was to invite Kevin Ward much to the chagrin of my daughter Rebecca. 'What about me?' she pleadingly quizzed.

'No sorry love, I'm taking Kevin.'

A subsequent phone call to Kevin revealed he could not make that date but a couple of weeks later would be fine. Consequently, with a little influence, my son Dean arranged a convenient July date, Friday the 10th, which ironically was the Castleford Tigers V St Helens match. Two of the big man's former clubs would be locking horns and we would be there to watch the game live.

The 10th soon came around, Kevin had queried what attire would be appropriate, I had replied, 'It will be warm Kevin, so I reckon a casual shirt and slacks will be suitable.' Together we left my home at around 5 o'clock in the evening courtesy of a lift by my wife Mavis. Rebecca was also in attendance, our PA for the evening. It was very warm, the sun still high as we sped along Aberford Road passing the St Peters estate and Moorhouse, childhood homes to both Kevin and myself. It is difficult to pass through these areas without some momentary fond memory triggering a flurry of conversation between us and so the mood was jovial as the car turned right down Newmarket Lane. Within seconds, we passed the former residence of the now nonexistent Newmarket Silkstone Collieries manager, where a recent modernisation has enhanced the already imposing facade of this Victorian mini-mansion. To the right a pair of impressive houses, both once inhabited by the two pit under managers. Their vast gardens partially hidden by large ash and oak trees confirmed my childhood memories of the posh yet foreboding nature of these symbolic residencies of yesteryear. On the left I spied the long row of deceptively large terrace houses that were once home to the mine's middle class white collar staff, the pecking order explained to me by my father so long ago was still plainly obvious. Our former estates, the Moorhouse and St Peters, are approximately one mile away on what was once a prime orchard site of the local manorial Moorhouse. Dad always explained, 'Just far enough away from the mine and the hierarchies residences so as not to interfere or intimidate, yet close enough to walk to work within minutes.'

As we travelled on Kevin glanced either side at the old pit site, silent and overgrown, masking the fact that the Newmarket shaft on the left hand side and the Monkey shaft on the right ever existed. Gone are the pit winding houses, the rail crossings, the coal hoppers, the noisy hubbub of steam locomotives and the blackened figures still wearing kneepads and carrying their lamps. Kevin commented: 'They would be making their way to the bathhouse on the Newmarket side.' He then recalled he too trod those same ghostly paths.

I remember walking with my dad up to the pay office on a Friday lunchtime, it was a two weekly ritual, he would be going on the afternoon shift. Dad would emerge from the pay office with a transparent envelope in hand which he would firmly place in my open outstretched palm, already perspiring through fear of the responsibility. It seems an irony that on the approach to the mine he would clasp my hand from leaving home to arriving at the pit gates, and then send me on the return journey alone. On reaching the pit gates I would nervously turn and wave, this after Dad had given me the usual stern lecture: 'Don't stop for nowt or nobody till tha gets to thi muther son, it took me a whole week to addle yon.' Then as soon as I was out of sight, I mounted my imaginary trusted steed. 'Yah! Yah!' I would holler as I broke into a stride that would increase into a sprint at the sight of my mother standing outside Walt Howe's shop on the entrance to that hallowed estate. I would be sweating profusely as I tied up trigger and handed the loot into Mum's grateful hand. 'You're a good lad our David an you can have a stick of Spanish as reward.'

I remember being quick to remind mum: 'Dad says a can have a tanner for t'clog (the local cinema) tonight Mam as well as.' Our mums would then buy the weekly groceries, watching and accounting for every penny. Dad would return home at 10 pm, the rest of his wage, apart from one and thrupence for Mr Sweet the insurance man, still intact.

'Old Sweety, old Arthur,' Kevin interjects, 'he was our insurance man.'

'I think he was everyone's insurance man Kevin.'

'Is he still alive Dave?'

'No he died a few years ago but Alan Parker is still living.'

This brings a broad smile to Kevin's features. 'Old Alan

Parker, helluva teacher he was Dave.'

It seems ironic that Kevin speaks so endearingly about an old former woodwork master who chastised him hard and often. It certainly pours scorn on the advocates who fought to abolish corporal punishment in schools as Kevin, who is a generation after myself argued, 'I only ever got what I deserved, it did me no long term damage, on the contrary, it taught me respect toward others.'

I feel filled with a warm glow as we manoeuvre the twists and turns of Newmarket lower lanes. Kevin strikes up, 'I used to say to my mam, "Mi dad says I can have a tanner," mum would snap in reply, "You'll get your dad says, here take this three penny bit and I'll give you another in mornin."' Then Kevin laughs, 'We used to run t'shop and spend it straight away.'

The former colliery site vanishes in our wake as the winding lane straightens out and we pass under the M62 motorway. 'Can you recall when the river burst its banks and all this were flooded Kev?'

'I certainly can, I was only young but I remember.'

'Well our Malc was called out by the brewery to the Bush pub, Old Bert and his wife were up in their bedroom. Our Malc rescued the dog downstairs, it was swimming in little circles with an outstretched lead fastened by the loop grip, Old Bert said he tied it up every night it was so nasty.'

'I'll bet it was glad to see your kid.'

'Well you would think so, another four inch of water and the poor bugger would have drowned but it was still snarling at our kid.'

'Ungrateful mutt.' Kevin concluded.

The Jungle was by now clearly in view ahead and small pockets of fans were slowly meandering along Wheldon Road. The faint aroma of onions and hot dogs wafted through our open windows as Mavis halted outside the main Arthur Atkinson memorial gate. We thanked Mavis for the lift and as we approached our entrance on foot, Tony Marchant hailed Kevin and jogged the few metres from the training field to greet us. Tony still looks exceptionally fit and well and his genuine friendship shines through, as my mind once again raced back through time when Kevin's sublime short pass as he burst the opposition at Wembley 1986, unleashed Tony on his spectacular seventy-metre run for his try. Tony returns to his charges in the under 18 squad who, much under strength he informs us, are to play a curtain raiser kicking off at 5.45 pm against a very strong Saints under 18s. On entering the ground Stan Wall is the first to greet Kevin. Stan one of the St Helens coaching staff, is on his way to join the Saints youngsters warming up. Kevin takes a deep breath and views the many changes that have taken place since the inception of Super League and the onset of the Jungle, then we wander round to the bar. Becky gets the drinks in, she orders a pint of lager for me then she turns to Kevin, 'What you drinking Kevin?'

Kevin stands facing the bar, his huge imposing frame appears to intimidate the barmaid, 'A pint of bitter please.'

'Would you like ordinary or extra cold?' the barmaid asks.

'What's the difference?' Kevin queries.

The girl looks at me then returns her gaze to Kevin, 'Well one's colder than the other sir!'

'I know that, I meant in price.'

'Oh no difference,' she sighs in relief.

'I'll have extra cold then, thanks,' states Kevin.

We are soon into our second pint when I ask Kevin, 'Why did you never pursue a career in coaching?'

'Because I was out of the game for two and a half years trying to recover from my injury, then when I realised my career had finished I enrolled on a bricklaying course to ensure some kind of future. With all the hours of rehabilitation on my leg I never had a chance, time out of the game you know what I mean?'

'Sure I do Kevin, you got left behind but you were years as a labourer on the building sites then when you left rugby you trained up to be a brickie, so why not apply the same to rugby?'

'Because father time has caught up with me now. I'm forty-eight next month.'

'I know Kev, it's my birthday the day after yours.'

Becky now informs us we are due up in the restaurant and as we stroll across a few of the security staff begin nudging and whispering. 'That big bugger's Kevin Ward,' one says. His mate quietly replies, 'No it's not.' I turn, smile and nod my head mouthing the words, 'It is, it is'.

Together we climb the steps up to the restaurant where we are greeted warmly by our host Russell Gaunt, who kindly guides us to the bar and further drinks. A faint aroma tells me that curry is on the menu, this information I pass to Kevin who bursts into laughter at what is a very private joke. Mike fires a quizzical look as if to say, was it something I said? So I quickly put him at ease explaining that this is my first proper meal since Wednesday evening, I have been on laxatives for two days to prepare my bowels for the barium enema X-ray I had undergone earlier in the day. Obviously Kevin had made the curry connection and it amused him, just as it did Mike following my explanation. But the meal was superb, Kevin and myself were looked after with warm hospitality by the other diners at our table which was sponsored by Wakefield Office Supplies. Kevin's opening statement was that he was surprised they were not Wakefield Wildcats supporters, but a tactful answer explained that it was off-the-field happenings which had persuaded them to transfer their allegiance.

That evening Kevin had agreed to take part in a question and answer session and when he was announced to the audience in the restaurant he received a tremendous ovation. He was bold enough to predict a Saints win, which I thought was very brave considering we were enjoying Castleford hospitality, then when one fan announced that Cas fans hate Leeds but how did Kevin feel about them? Kevin replied tongue in cheek, 'We all hate Leeds,' which was received with cheers and a round of applause.

But it was all good harmless banter which Mick Morgan finished by adding an original amusing ditty to conclude our pre-match hospitality.

We headed for our seats in the main stand despite constantly being stopped for a courteous handshake or pat on the back. 'If he wants to come in I'm not going to try stopping him,' quipped the security man laughingly. On finally settling in our seats a small boy a few rows away was awe-struck and with a bottom jaw agape he attempted to swivel his dad's head a full turn. 'Look Dad,' he said in a hardly audible whisper, 'it's the Hulk.' The game was about to start yet the disinterested parent finally turned his head in a nonchalant manner but then his eyes widened when he recognised Kevin. 'That's Kevin Ward, silly boy, he was better than the Hulk,' he stated. 'Oh cool!' replied the boy. He was to receive the big man's autograph later, a trait that endeared Kevin during his heyday as he always had time for the fans, it was never too much trouble to spend time or sign autographs for his legions of admirers.

As for the game, it was fast and ferocious with St Helens hitting their straps in magnificent style. Their Aussie prop, Darren Brit, looked every inch a world-class player, his hard fearless running tore holes in the feeble Cas midfield and defence. It was eerily reminiscent of the big man sat on my left in his halcyon days. Then at half-time, Kevin added to the on field entertainment when he was invited on to the pitch to talk to the crowd while the stewards set up the staging of the 'Win a Car' competition. Kevin was invited to have a go after the lucky punters had taken part and he narrowly missed - the closest anyone had come that evening. Then both sets of supporters showed their affection when they sang, 'There's only one Kevin Ward,' followed by the chant of 'Wardie, Wardie, Wardie,' as Kevin returned to his seat. Few men with these two clubs could have generated such warmth, such admiring adoration a decade after they had played their final game. When he sat back beside me it hit home that I was alongside a true icon in the history of rugby league, our great game. Kevin, in typical fashion, enthused only about narrowly missing out on the free car. 'I almost had it, I almost had it.' The exercise had been to kick a rugby ball through a hole between giant inflatable imitation rugby posts. When Kevin calmly stroked the ball with a sweet-as-you-like left foot, I was instantly reminded of his youth, an aspiring soccer star with genuine potential who, like many others over the years, lacked the courage to leave their little parochial hamlets to take up the opportunity of a lifetime. Then the second half kicks off and I realise Kevin was different to most. He came to his senses, found the courage and lifted his community to his level rather than allow it to swallow him.

The second stanza proved equally exciting as the first with Kevin showing enthusiasm for both teams' successes. He mentioned that Cas lacked an enforcer up front, he was impressed with the pace of Darren Albert, the silky skills of Shaun Long and excited at the power of Keiron Cunningham, who burst through and clear before handing on to the ever supporting and opportunistic Micky Higham. In this rich vein of form Saints were irrepressible but Kevin very fairly pointed out that Cas were valiant in defeat, scoring the try of the match and the last one of the day. The final score line of 46-32 was a fair indication of Saints' superiority on the night and Cas's battling spirit.

After the game we headed to the bar for our post match tipple. Kevin was eager to meet faces from the past but things are nowadays much changed at the Jungle and many of the faces he sought are no longer there. 'Thirteen years is a long time,' I remind him. The disappointment is clearly etched in his expression, broken only occasionally by some well-meaning well-wisher from the past. We were joined by my son Dean, his long day over, and then by a dejected looking Cas coach, Graham Steadman. Graham greeted Kevin, Dean and myself with a startling and much appreciated statement, 'I could have done with you three out there today.'

Kevin replied, 'I wish I could have been there for you mate.'

We were unified in our opinion of where Cas were lacking on the night, despite such a brave effort. Over the next couple of pints the conversation ebbed and flowed but Kevin obviously found it increasingly difficult to comprehend the lack of the presence of ex-players, he also puzzled as to the whereabouts of many long-standing loyal cliques of fans who were at one time included on the inventory of fixtures and fittings. I explained to him that many ceased with the advent of Super League, unable to accept the changes it brought.

'Such as?' Kevin asked.

'Several factors, I suppose with the disco culture that evolved people can't have the in depth conversations like before so they give the bar a miss. Others complained about the predictability of the pattern of every game. Some could not accept the blind eye turned to basics, which they had come to expect for years. And probably a few must have passed on to the great hereafter. Anyway, some of the refs don't help either.'

'No, there's too much confusion and no consistency. Look at that game a few weeks back when Dennis Moran was obstructed for London Broncos in the dying seconds against Hull. That should have been a penalty, no wonder some fans get upset.' Kevin said.

'That's true but fortunately new converts are being recruited to replace the ones deserting.'

'I suppose it's called progress Dave.'

'You're right Kev but think just how much progress could be really made if we retained those old fans and still added the converts.'

Our voices were now raised competing with the disco so we reluctantly moved outside, then Becky informed us that our taxi awaited. For myself I felt fine, I had had a wonderful evening, Kevin concurred. Neither of us were intoxicated, just talkative and perhaps a little tired.

'How many before you think it's home time these days Kevin?' I asked.

'Oh, just a few, I don't drink as much now.'

'Yes, me too,' I added.

'It was your fault we used to drink too much anyway Sammy, you weaned us.'

'Oh thanks a lot Kevin, blame me, everyone does.'

The taxi soon covered the seven miles and I bid Kevin and Dean goodnight, it had been a wonderful evening out, I can recommend it, a little positive nostalgia never hurts.

Postscript

In the final analysis, now the dust has settled and the leg has finally healed, at least as much as it ever will, it is a far wiser Kevin Ward who has emerged. He knows there were mistakes made at the time of his injury that have physically and mentally scarred him for life, but he states the most frustrating thing was at the time, having no redress. 'Oh I have countless fond memories,' he states, 'and I'm grateful I was able to enjoy such a long and rewarding career during which I made friends with so many fans, officials and players from opposite sides of the world. Even long after my enforced retirement, people wrote to me from the least expected places wishing me well, all of them comforting and inspirational.'

'Didn't that make you bitter about your injury and all the things that went wrong in your treatment?' I asked.

'It did at first, I started legal action to claim for some kind of compensation but the bitterness wore off and I just let the matter drop.'

I once asked Kevin to sum up in one word why he was so successful on the rugby pitch. His response was typical:

'Gameness Dave, gameness.'

'I'm not sure I understand.'

'Well I don't know if it's a real word or even if it is, I don't know if the dictionary definition is the same as mine, but I reckon if two teams are equal in every department, right down to the last detail, there's one factor that will separate them.'

'Gameness?' I questioned.

'That's right, gameness, and that was my biggest attribute, I could not be out gamed, I always tried to play at least as well as my opponent and you could bet if I was running on low he was running on empty, I was always able to dip into reserves he didn't have.'

For me, these comments sum up the characteristics of Kevin, whilst he always gives his best - and he played a damn hard game of rugby in his day - he nevertheless does not bear grudges when things don't work out as planned. Maybe some people think he is a little soft or a bit of a pushover, but I think he's just a big tough capable man with the strength to take everything on the chin. It's true to say he was lucky enough to be born with the skills and physical characteristics to play rugby at the very highest level, but that's not enough; plenty of people are born with the potential to become sporting greats. The difference is that just a few have the desire to succeed and are prepared to make the huge effort to make sure they do. For my part, I'm just happy that I've been able to have an influence on his career in those early days when I encouraged him to take up rugby league and then when I asked Castleford to take a look at him, which set him off on his professional career. And, I am again proud that I've been asked to write his story and tell his great adventure, so I guess I was there at the start and I am here at the end, which seems kind of fitting. One thing I do reflect on though is that I would have been much happier if Kevin had been able to voluntarily hang up his boots at the end of his career with a Premiership winner's medal or even just a wave goodbye to the fans at an end of a season game. Whereas to conclude his career in the manner he did seems so brutal and unfair, but I guess the positive side is it now adds a great deal to his story, so maybe every cloud has a silver lining, at least in part.

Well that's Kevin's story, love him or not, he deserves an enormous amount of recognition and I'm sure all his team-mates and his opponents from his halcyon days at Castleford, Manly and St Helens still respect him. From his humble beginnings, he embarked on a great adventure, which took him around the world and made him one of the all-time great rugby league players and a true sporting icon. He had a little help along the way, his team-mates, the inspirational Mal Reilly, Bobby Fulton, Mike McClennan and not least, his wife Margaret, but he achieved the bulk of it by himself with the long hours of training and his efforts on the pitch which won him accolades far and wide. And at the end of his career, when the chips were down, he fought back from adversity to at least give himself the dignity of being able to earn a working wage – a man that truly lives by the principle of no pain, no gain.

Appendix - Kevin Ward Rugby League Statistics

Castleford

Signed 14th of November 1978, from Stanley Rangers.
Debut (as a sub) V Salford (away), 14th of March 1979, Lost 15-6.
Last match (as a sub) V Leeds (away), 22nd of April 1990, Lost 18-24.

Season	Apps	Subs	Tries	Pts
1978/79	3	1	0	0
1979/80	25	1	11	33
1980/81	33	0	13	39
1981/82	25	0	13	39
1982/83	28	1	10	30
1983/84	29	0	6	24
1984/85	26	1	7	28
1985/86	34	0	3	12
1986/87	25	2	3	12
1987/88	25	1	4	16
1988/89	28	2	2	8
1989/90	23	3	2	8
Total	304	12	74	249

Honours

1979/80: 2 GB under 24 appearances
1980/81: 2 GB under 24 appearances

1981/82: Yorkshire Cup (win & 1 try); 1 appearance Yorkshire
1983/84: Premiership (runner-up); 1 appearance GB
1985/86: Yorkshire Cup (runner-up); Challenge Cup (win)
1986/87: Yorkshire Cup (win); Charity Shield (runner-up); 3 GB appearances
1987/88: Yorkshire Cup (runner-up); 1 Yorkshire, 7 GB & Tour, 1 ROW appearances
1988/89: Yorkshire Cup (runner-up); 2 GB & 1 ROW appearances

St Helens
Signed 6th of June 1990.
Debut (Lancashire Cup) V Trafford Borough (home), 16th of July 1990, Won 56-24.
Last match V Wigan (away), 9th of April 1993, Drew 8-8.

Season	Apps	Sub	Tries	Pts
1990/91	30	0	2	8
1991/92	35	0	3	12
1992/93	21	3	3	12
Total	86	3	8	32

Honours
1990/91: Challenge Cup (runner-up); 2 GB Subs
1991/92: Lancashire Cup (win); Premiership Trophy (runner-up)
1992/93: Charity Shield (win); Lancashire Cup (runner-up); 1 GB World Cup Final appearance

Manly
Signed May 1987.
Debut V Balmain (home), 24th of May 1987, won 48-14.
Last match Grand Final (Winfield Cup) V Canberra at SCG, 27th of September 1987, won 18-8.

Season	Apps	Sub	Tries	Pts
1987	11	1	1	4
1988 *(after GB tour)*	4	0	1	4
Total	15	1	2	8

Honours
1987: Winfield Cup (win)

Yorkshire Appearances

Year	Venue	Versus	Position	Result
1982	Leigh	Lancs	13, 1 try	Won 22-21
1987	Wigan	Lancs	8	Won 16-10

Great Britain Appearances

Year	Venue	Versus	Position	Result
1984	Leeds	France	10	Won 10-0
1986	Old Trafford	Aus	8	Lost 16-38
1986	Elland Road	Aus	8	Lost 4-34
1986*	Wigan	Aus	8	Lost 15-24
1987	Wigan	Papua	8	Won 42-8
1988	Avignon	France	8	Won 28-14
1988	Leeds	France	8	Won 30-12
1988*	Port Moresby	Papua	8	Won 42-22
1988	Sydney	Aus	8	Lost 6-17
1988	Brisbane	Aus	8	Lost 14-34
1988*	Sydney	Aus	8	Won 26-12
1988*	Christchurch	NZ	8	Lost 10-12
1989	Wigan	France	8	Won 26-10
1989	Avignon	France	8	Won 30-8
1990	Wembley	Aus	15	Won 19-12
1990	Old Trafford	Aus	15	Lost 10-14
1992**	Wembley	Aus	8	Lost 6-10

*World Cup   ** World Cup Final

1988 Tour (Non Tests)

Date	Opponents	Position	Result
June 1st	Newcastle Knights	8, 1 try	Won 28-12
June 17th	Central Queensland	8	Won 64-8
June 22nd	Toowoomba	8	Won 28-12
July 5th	Presidents XIII	8	Lost 16-24
July 19th	Auckland	8	Lost 14-30

Two additional international appearances, one for GB V Rest of World, one for Rest of World V Australia.

Stats Totals

Club	Apps	Sub	Tries	Points
Castleford	304	12	74	249
St Helens	86	3	8	32
Manly	15	1	2	8
Yorkshire	2	0	1	3
Tour (NT)	5	1	1	4
Rest of World	1	0	1	4
GB V ROW	1	0	0	0
GB Tests	15	2	0	0
Un 24s Int	3	0	0	0
Total	432	19	87	300